JOSÉ MARIA SISON

REFLECTIONS ON REVOLUTION AND PROSPECTS

Interviews by Rainer Werning

With a foreword by E. San Juan, Jr.

Julieta de Lima
Editor

International Network for Philippine Studies
The Netherlands

ISBN 978-1-62847-937-9

9 781628 479379

Published by

International Network for Philippine Studies (INPS)

ISBN 978-1-62847-937-9

Cover by Jon Bustamante

Book design by Alvin Firmeza

Contents

Foreword

by E. San Juan, Jr.[1]

Writing for the Madrid journal *La Solidaridad* in 1889, a decade before the United States occupied the Philippines as its new possession, José Rizal surmised in his essay "Filipinas dentro de cien años": "Perhaps the great American Republic, whose interests lie in the Pacific and who has no hand in the spoliation of Africa may some day dream of foreign possession...." But if she did, even contrary to her tradition, the European powers would forbid it, and if the United States tried to, "Very likely the Philippines will defend with inexpressible valor the liberty secured at the price of so much blood and sacrifice." (1972, 127). Rizal's uncanny presentiment was a warning: the natives resisted McKinley's "Benevolent Assimilation" and US "tutelage" from 1898 on. They persevered up to the Sakdal and Huk uprisings, and the ongoing resistance of the National Democratic Front and its national-popular combatants.

Under the aegis of global capitalism's "war against terrorism," the carnage has worsened in the longest-held US neocolony in Asia since its annexation at the turn of the last century. After 9/11, US imperial subjugation of the Philippines intensified with successive counterinsurgency schemes dating back to the Cold War. Beyond the three million Filipinos killed by US troops in the Filipino-American War (1899-1913, dubbed the "first Vietnam"), thousands died in the bloody years of the Marcos dictatorship (1972-1986) supported by Washington and the Pentagon (Ahmad 1971; Zinn 1984).

We are witness to current US interventions via the Visiting Forces Agreement, Enhanced Defense Cooperation Agreement (EDCA), Operation Pacific Eagle-Philippines, and other bilateral transactions to preserve US neocolonial domination. This includes supply of

1 E.San Juan, Jr. is emeritus professor of Comparative Literature, University of Connecticut, USA; visiting professor of English, University of the Philippines; former fellow, W.E.B. Du Bois Institute, Harvard University and Fulbright professor of American Studies, Leuven University, Belgium; professorial chairholder, Polytechnic University of the Philippines, editorial adviser for the journals *CULTURAL LOGIC*, *KritikaKultura*, *Unitas*, *Humanities Diliman*, *Malay*, and *Bisig*.

weaponry, logistics, and supervision over the Armed Forces of the Philippines (AFP). This was recently demonstrated by the US participation in the devastation of Marawi City in 2017. Without US stranglehold of key ideological state apparatuses implementing IMF/World Bank/WTO regulations, the local oligarchy of landlords, compradors, and bureaucrat-capitalists from 1899 to 1972—as José Maria Sison has expounded in *Philippine Society and Revolution* (PSR)—would not survive.

Sison is universally recognized as a pertinacious radical leader of the Filipino contingent challenging US imperialism. His signal accomplishment, in my view, is his cogent re-telling of the narrative of the Filipino national-liberation odyssey in PSR, updated in 1986.[2] Of exceeding importance is Julieta de Lima's perspicuous thematic inquiry of this narrative in "José Maria Sison on the Mode of Production" (Sison and De Lima 1988).[3] Earlier attempts have been made by Apolinario Mabini, Claro Recto, Teodoro Agoncillo, Renato Constantino, among others. But only with PSR did the Filipino masses finally acquire a counter-hegemonic voice, freeing the energies of its long-repressed incarnate Geist, and enabling the rekindling of revolutionary agency. Of course, world events, in particular the 1955 Bandung Conference, the Cuban Revolution, the 1965-68 Cultural Revolution in China, the Civil Rights struggle in the US coinciding with worldwide resistance against US aggression in Vietnam, and the resurgence of the patriotic movement in the 1970 "First Quarter Storm," etc.—all these and more provided fertile ground for its germination.

In 1968, Sison broke away from the old Soviet-inspired Communist Party initially led by Crisanto Evangelista and Pedro Abad Santos. Its caretakers (the Lava brothers, etc.) easily succumbed to the Marcos regime. Humans make history but not under circumstances of their choosing. Sison undertook the necessary critical inventory[4] and

---

2 See "Lectures on Philippine Crisis and Revolution" in *Selected Writings, 1968-1991: Continuing the Struggle for National and Social Liberation (1986-1991), 2013, pp. 61-141.*-Editor

3 Also in *Selected Writings, 1968-1991: Detention and Defiance against Dictatorship (1977-1986), 2013, pp. 399-446.*-Editor

4 See "Rectify Errors and Rebuild the Party" in *Selected Writings, 1968-1991: Foundation for Resuming the Philippine Revolution (1968-1972), 2013, pp. 5-58* and *Selected Writings, 1968-1991: Defeating Revisionism, Reformism and Opportunism (1969-1974)*, 2013.-Editor

launched a rectification campaign that led to the re-establishment of the Communist Party of the Philippines (CPP) by Sison and his comrades in 1968. It was preceded by his formation of Kabataang Makabayan [Patriotic Youth] in November 1964. The concept of united front in the national-democratic, anti-imperialist campaign acquired saliency, accompanied by a regeneration of commitment to the ideals of emancipatory praxis. The new CPP was inspired by Mao's vision of conducting people's war in a non-European setting. What was at stake was not a set of dogmas or personality-cult but a model of guidelines or methods for testing hypotheses and applying Marxist-Leninist principles on the historical specificities of the Philippine socioeconomic formation (see "Programme for a People's Democratic Revolution in the Philippines"[5] (Saulo 1990, 196-209; San Juan 2015).

Curiously enough, the US State Department 1950 report on the Huk insurgency concurs with Sison's re-emphasis on the central role of the peasantry in elucidating the feudal/landlord problem (1987). Just as Mao renewed Marxist dialectics in his 1927 investigation of the Hunan peasant movement, Sison's reappraisal of the diverse political forces involved in the unremitting class struggle from Spanish times to the present revitalized historical-materialist thinking applied to Philippine reality. He tested Lenin's methodology of concrete analysis of historically dynamic situations, focused on "the weak links," which led to Lenin's insight into the decisive role of national liberation struggles in catalyzing the Western proletariat's internationalist mission (1968). He examined the historical particularities of crucial conjunctures in the saga of our uneven development. What proved to be decisive was the revaluation of the strategy and tactics of the class struggle with the founding of the New People's Army on March 29, 1969, and the application of Mao Zedong's theory of protracted war pursuing various interlocking stages of the revolutionary process (Ch'en 1965; Rossanda 1970).

The next historic milestone in Sison's contribution to the Marxist archive is the 1974 discourse on "Specific Characteristics of Our People's War."[6] Sison was arrested by the Marcos regime in 1977 and endured torture and other indignities until its overthrow in February

5 In *Selected Writings, 1968-1991: Foundation for Resuming the Philippine Revolution (1968-1972), 2013, pp. 59-77.*-Editor

6 In *Selected Writings, 1968-1991: Building Strength through Struggle (1972-1977), 2013, pp. 179-217.*-Editor

1986. He has described this ordeal and its aftermath in his poems, letters, interviews, and other essays collected in *Detention and Defiance against Dictatorship* (2013). After the US debacle in Vietnam and at the height of the Cultural Revolution in China, the gains of the CPP and New People's Army made possible the reaffirmation of the Filipino struggle as part of the radical democratic-socialist transformations around the world initiated by the 1917 Russian revolution.

Historians have argued that instead of homogenizing the planet, capitalism generates zones of differences, asymmetrical or disaggregated networks of actions and motivations that defy synthesis. Unity and conflict of opposites prevail. While the 1930 Depression stimulated union organizing among migrant workers of Bulosan's generation, the Japanese Occupation taught the peasants the various modes of guerrilla warfare and collective mobilization. The Cold War from the 1950s to the collapse of the Soviet Union in 1991 ushered the need for an uninterrupted, all-encompassing Cultural Revolution. What is original in Sison's 1974 discourse is the re-articulation of the country's historical peculiarities in line with the national-democratic program: the mountainous archipelagic terrain, the dialectic of rural and urban zones, and in particular the contours of strategic defensive-stalemate-offensive stages in the uninterrupted transition from a feudal-bourgeois to a new-democratic formation. Following this trajectory, the National Democratic Front Philippines, founded in 1973, issued the 10-Point[7] (later 12-Point) program, which informs the ultimate agenda of the peace talks.

In 1988, Rainer Werning conducted a wide-ranging series of interviews with Sison in *The Philippine Revolution: The Leader's View.* Sison's travels around the world interacting with various progressive organizations afforded him opportunities to connect the Philippine project with other third-world and European solidarity movements. Before that, in 1980, we were able to arrange the publication of Sison's other writings in the volume *Victory to Our People's War* released in Quebec, Canada.

With the next historic intervention in 1992, "Reaffirm our Basic Principles and Rectify Errors," Sison demonstrated once again his grasp of a dialectical analysis of the interaction of strategy and tactics, fallibilistic hypotheses and contingencies, enabling a grasp of

---

[7] Ibid., *pp. 133-147.*-Editor

the multilayered contradictions in the vicissitudes of the national-democratic endeavor. By refusing the empiricist or eclectic position of his critics, Sison has applied the concept of the unity of opposites as the fundamental law of dialectical materialism, a concept which Mao first addressed in the classic 1937 discourse, "On Contradiction" (elaborated further in the 1957 talk, "On the Correct Handling of Contradictions Among the People" (1977, 384-419; see Knight 1997, 104). Failure to recognize the unity and antagonism of opposites has led to various "Left" and Right opportunist lines (pacifism, revisionist compromises, etc.), including collusion with reactionary security agencies and CIA counterinsurgency schemes (Distor 1977). The bankruptcy of such deviations has been evidenced in the spectacle of former leftists functioning as apologists of US neoliberal policies, with assorted NGOs set up to serve the corrupt oligarchy (landlords, compradors) managing the neocolonial State bureaucracy.

Sison's vocation as a Filipino advocate for national sovereignty and human rights in the diaspora has opened a new field of internationalist contestation. Over ten million Overseas Filipino Workers (OFWs) are scattered today around the world, forcing candidates for office to campaign in Hong Kong, Singapore, in the Middle East, etc. Their remittances are significant in relieving the Philippine foreign debt as well as intensifying commodity-fetishism, alienation, and consumerist decadence. Meanwhile, Filipino activists are politicizing these communities in the US, Europe, and in the Netherlands where Sison has been a political refugee since 1988. Apart from his imprisonment by the Marcos regime, his detention by the Dutch government in August 28, 2007 until September 13, 2007, for unsubstantiated charges has made Sison a symbol of all the thousands victimized by the US imperial "war on terror." Since 2001 he has guided the International League of People's Struggles, the biggest international united front of people's organizations along the anti-imperialist and democratic line.

One of the most instructive sections of these interviews is Sison's insightful critique of the neocolonial administrations since the fall of Marcos up to the current fascist Duterte regime. His discussion of the impact of global changes on the Philippine system, in particular the capitalist restoration in the former Soviet Union and in China, as well as the decline of US global hegemony, gives us the framework for speculations on the prospects of the Philippine revolution amidst a worldwide socialist resurgence. Again, the focus is on the exploited and oppressed, the community of victims, workers and peasants whose narratives remain to be written. With the assassination of NDFP consultant Felix Malayao and the arrest of other progressive activists at the behest of US imperialist agencies, Sison believes a peace agreement is unlikely—unless the revolutionary mass movement unleashes its counter-hegemonic force against Duterte's murderous regime, with its horrendous record of extrajudicial killings and betrayal of the nation's patrimony and sovereignty.

Equally fascinating in this volume is Sison's reflections on diverse topics as a Filipino patriot, chief political consultant of the NDFP, and as an intransigent Marxist public intellectual. Sison invokes his descent from the first Filipino socialist agitator, Isabelo de Los Reyes, who organized the first labor unions and also co-founded the nationalistic Iglesia Filipina Independiente (IFI). He pays homage to the Enlightenment tradition of de los Reyes, Rizal, Mabini and others which the Chinese patriot Sun Yat-sen had the sagacity to admire. Sison sums up his legacy "in the form of theoretical and political writings needed for the reestablishment and development of the CPP as a revolutionary party of the proletariat and for the creation and growth of all other necessary revolutionary forces, including the NPA, the NDFP, the mass organizations and the people's democratic government from the village level upward." Indeed, this legacy today continues to be a powerful challenge to predatory capitalism worldwide, a "disintegrated capitalism" wreaking havoc on the environment and mutilating the lives of millions, unable to resolve the contradictions inherent in the system and therefore destined to either destroy the planet or be thoroughly replaced by a socialist/communist alternative (Harvey 2014).

Overall, this volume contains the most important record of Sison's life based on his prodigious memory and ability to contextualize the most significant events shaping his thoughts and actions. It contributes substantial information on his education, political inquiries, and the scope and depth of his artistic creativity. It also documents his timely interventions into the most pivotal moments of our history. It gives a nuanced orchestration to his dialogue with his European interviewer. I am sure it will furnish material for future biographies and commentaries on the symbiosis of human will and objective circumstances. However, to anticipate the chances that the reader may miss the historic resonance of these interviews, I would like to add a personal note. We (if I may speak for our group of militants in the East Coast circa 1965-80) read Marx, Lenin, Mao, Luxemburg, Fanon, Lukács, Che Guevara, and others before we encountered PSR. We were then trying to mobilize the "brainwashed" Filipino community in the US against Marcos' barbaric rule, his violation of human rights, his opening the country to foreign corporate plunder, etc. It was difficult until PSR provided a clue to arousing the historical consciousness of young Pinoys/Pinays. And so we began to retell the story of Lapu-Lapu, Gabriela Silang, Gomburza, Bonifacio, Sakay, Salud Algabre, Teresa Magbanua, Maria Lorena Barros, and countless heroic protagonists of our history.

"Only connect," as the saying goes. We thus succeeded in organizing rallies and learning/teaching seminars, lobbying legislators to cut off military aid to Marcos, supporting multi-ethnic farm workers exploited by the same corporations pillaging their homeland, and other activities. We also used Carlos Bulosan's works together with the testimonies of Filipino unionists who spearheaded dangerous strikes in the fields of Hawaii and California. PSR then afforded us an excellent pedagogical instrument which sparked the conscientization (Paulo Freire's term) of almost two generations of activists in the US and elsewhere. PSR is now a legendary document that, contextualized in its milieu and with reference to Sison's whole career, can be more justly appreciated as a contribution to the advance of counter-hegemonic, national-popular movements around the world.

The Filipino people today, with their long durable tradition of anti-colonial and anti-feudal resistance, find themselves at a crossroad. The moribund system in its convulsive death-pangs eviscerates both victims and victimizers. The global crisis is worsening every day. Profit accumulation by finance capital signifies prolonging and aggravating underdevelopment—the poverty and misery of millions—particularly in the non-industrialized, neocolonized regions such as the Philippines. The Permanent Peoples' Tribunal held in The Hague in 2007, which Rainer Werning and I attended, pronounced the US-Arroyo regime guilty of massive crimes, among them untold cases of extrajudicial killings, torture, enforced disappearances, barbaric brutalities with impunity—communities destroyed or dispersed, millions of lives wasted (for Marcos' crimes, see McCoy 2011). The verdict declared that the systematic violations of the rights of the Filipino people, their sovereignty and integrity, by the Bush and Arroyo governments are crimes against humanity. The Tribunal also condemned those powers that "under the pretext of the so-called 'war on terrorism' and in the mantle of 'market- and profit-driven globalization'—deprive the marginalized of a life in justice, dignity, and peace" (San Juan 2007, 252-53).

History unfortunately seems to repeat itself. On 19 September 2018, this same Tribunal after days of sifting the evidence and hearing oral testimonies, arrived at a verdict sounding much the same as the 2007 one, this time the defendants on trial were Philippine President Rodrigo Roa Duterte and US President Donald Trump. They were found guilty of "gross and systematic violations of civil, political, economic, social and cultural rights, and "the rights of the people to national self-determination and development, the people's right to liberation" (Cohn 2019). Whether these outrages will continue for the next decades or so, barring ecological cataclysms, are the urgent questions to which Sison's interviews here can provide the answers if not the heuristic orientation necessary in clarifying what needs to be done. As we celebrate the golden anniversary of the founding of the New People's Army, and the 80th birthday of its founder, we forge our passage through the "labor of the negative," expressing here the travails and hopes of the proletarianized masses in the long march not to a proverbial utopia but to a sense of fulfilment in having affirmed our people's dignity, integrity, and inexhaustible creativity.

References

Ahmad, Eqbal. 1971. "The Theory and Fallacies of Counter-Insurgency." *The Nation* (August 1972): 19-26.

Ch'en, Jerome. 1965. *Mao and the Chinese Revolution*. New York: Oxford University Press.

Cohn, Marjorie. 2019. "Tribunal Declares Trump and Duterte Guilty of Crimes Against Humanity." *Truthout* (March 14). <http://truthout.org>

Communist Party of the Philippines. 1990. "Programme for a People's Democratic Revolution in the Philippines." In *Communism in the Philippines: An Introduction* by Alfredo Saulo. Quezon City: Ateneo de Manila University Press.

Distor, Emerita Dionisio. 1977. "Maoism and the Development of the Communist Party of the Philippines." *In Critical Perspectives on Mao Zedong's Thought*, ed. Arif Dirlik, Paul Healy and Nick Knight. New Jersey: Humanities Press.

Harvey, David. 2014. *Seventeen Contradictions and the End of Capitalism*. New York: Oxford University Press.

Knight, Nick. 1977. "The Laws of Dialectical Materialism in Mao Zedong's Thought: The Question of 'Orthodoxy'." In Critical *Perspectives on Mao Zedong's Thought.* New Jersey: Humanities Press.

Lenin, Vladimir. 1968. National Liberation, Socialism and Imperialism: *Selected Writings.* New York: International Publishers.

Mao Zedong. 1977. "On the Correct Handling of Contradictions Among the People." *Selected Works of Mao Tsetung. Volume V.* Peking: Foreign Languages Press.

McCoy, Alfred. 2011. "Dark Legacy: Human Rights under the Marcos Regime." *Memory, Truth Telling and the Pursuit of Justice: A Conference on the Legacies of the Marcos Dictatorship.* Ateneo de Manila University: Office of Research and Publications, pp. 129-144.

Rizal, José. 1979. "The Philippines A Century Hence" (Derbyshire translation). In *José Rizal.* Manila: National Historical Institute, pp. 96-129.

Rossanda, Rossana. 1971. "Mao's Marxism." *Socialist Register*: 53-80.

San Juan, E. 2007. *US Imperialism and Revolution in the Philippines.* New York: Palgrave Macmillan.

——. 2015. *Between Empire and Insurgency.* Quezon City: University of the Philippines Press.

Sison, José Maria [Amado Guerrero, pseudonym]. 1971. *Philippine Society and Revolution.* Manila: Pulang Tala.

——. [Amado Guerrero, pseudonym]. 1974. *Specific Characteristics of People's War in the Philippines.* Oakland, CA: International Association of Filipino Patriots.

——. 2013. *Selected Writings, 1968-1991: Detention and Defiance against Dictatorship, 1977 to 1986.* Manila: International Network for Philippines Studies and Aklat ng Bayan, Inc.

Sison, José Maria and Julieta de Lima. 1998. *Philippine Economy and Politics.* Manila: Aklat ng Bayan.

US State Dept. 1987. "The Hukbalahaps." In *The Philippines Reader,* ed. Daniel B. Schirmer and Stephen Shalom. Boston: South End Press, pp. 70-77.

Zinn, Howard. 1984. *The Twentieth Century.* New York: Harper.

★ ★ ★

Editor's Preface

Reflections on Revolution and Prospects is a book-length structured interview of José Maria Sison, Founding Chairman of the Communist Party of the Philippines (CPP) and Chairperson of the International League of Peoples' Struggle (ILPS) by his fellow political scientist Rainer Werning, a renowned scholarly expert on Philippine and East Asian politics and current affairs.

The interviewer and the interviewee succeed once more in using the format that they used in co-authoring an earlier work, *The Philippine Revolution: the Leader's View* in 1988, more than thirty years ago. Since then, tremendous events with significant implications and consequences have occurred in the world and in the Philippines.

Sison, the main subject of the book, has been widely recognized as an authority on these events as a public intellectual and analyst as well as a resolute and militant political actor, especially in the Philippines. He stands on the solid ground as the CPP founding chairman and ILPS chairperson when he speaks on Philippine and global issues.

The interviewer Rainer Werning reveals his expertise as a political scientist well-versed in global and Philippine affairs by raising profound and provocative questions on a comprehensive range of issues. Sison responds to his questions in an accurate and factual manner with insights borne of his long experience as a revolutionary thinker and leader.

Reflections on Revolution and Prospects presents a factual view of the background, the currents and the prospects of the epochal struggle between capitalism and socialism on the scale of the world and of the Philippines since 1988.

Sison's consistent thesis is that the full restoration of capitalism in former socialist countries since 1989-91 has increased the number of imperialist powers at the top of the world capitalist system, thus generating more crisis, state terrorism and wars of aggression.

The world is still in the era of modern imperialism and proletarian revolution, in accordance with the Marxist dictum since the time of Lenin. The danger and actuality of inter-imperialist wars are a prelude to revolutions for national liberation, democracy and socialism.

The socialist cause continues and its success in further rounds of socialist revolution is guaranteed by Mao's theory and practice of continuing revolution under the socialist state through a series of cultural revolutions in order to combat revisionism, prevent capitalist restoration and consolidate the gains of socialism.

Nowadays, it is observable that the "integrated capitalism" in the seventy years after World War II, including the restoration of capitalism in former socialist countries, is leading to "disintegrated capitalism" showing the same dangerous conditions that preceded the outbreaks of World War I and World War II. This time, the danger of nuclear war is looming.

Sison expresses the optimistic view that the worst consequence of monopoly capitalism, be it the threat of nuclear war due to inter-imperialist conflict or global warming due to corporate ruination of the environment, can be counteracted effectively only by the rise of the revolutionary mass movements led by proletarian parties in the developed and underdeveloped countries against imperialism and all reaction.

The significance and value of *Reflections on Revolution and Prospects* are enhanced by the insightful preface of E. San Juan, Jr., a world-renowned social and cultural analyst and critic. We thank him for expressing his overview of this book and the issues it covers. We also thank all other peers who have reviewed the manuscript and given valuable suggestions for its improvement.

For further information of readers, we have included as appendices the following: the brief biodata of Rainer Werning; the resume of José Maria Sison; the complete list of Sison's books; the resolutions of the Second National Congress of the Communist Party of the Philippines according him the highest honors, and of the ILPS Sixth International Assembly designating Sison as ILPS Chairperson Emeritus and a tribute by Lisa Ito of the Concerned Artists of the Philippines (CAP) read at the ceremony honoring Sison for his service to the ILPS and its anti-imperialist and democratic cause; a selection of his poems; and lastly some photographs relevant to each chapter of this book.

Julieta de Lima
Utrecht, The Netherlands
29 March 2019

Chapter I

Major changes in the world since 1989

1. Soon after your release from prison with the fall of the Marcos dictatorship, you went on a global lecture tour from 1986-1988. Could you tell me the global regions and particular countries you went to. What were the main features or highlights of these trips?

JMS: First of all, let me cite the countries to which I traveled during my global speaking tour, starting in the first week of September 1986. My tour was hectic and lasted for two years until September 1988 when my Philippine passport was cancelled by the Aquino government.

In the Asia-Pacific region, I went to Australia, New Zealand, Thailand, Japan, Hong Kong, India, China and the People's Democratic Republic of Korea. In Western Europe, I went to more than twenty countries. From Netherlands as my base, I traveled also to Algeria and Albania as well as to Latin America, particularly to Nicaragua, Cuba and Mexico. I was barred from going to the US to fulfill a series of ten lectures from coast to coast and to visit relatives and friends.

In most of the countries that I visited, I went to a number of cities to give university lectures mainly on the history, current circumstances and prospects of the Philippines and the Filipino people. Academics and nonacademics were interested in listening to my lectures because the Marcos fascist dictatorship had fallen only months before and I was seen as a major opponent of it.

I was also guest speaker in meetings organized by trade unions, solidarity organizations and Filipino communities. I met and conversed with government officials and the leaders of major political parties, various types of people's organizations and institutions interested in the Philippines.

For very specific reasons, I traveled to certain countries like Thailand, to receive the highest literary award in my home region, the Southeast Asia WRITE Award from the Thai Royal family; Algeria as guest of the Palestinian Parliament or the assembly of the National Council of the Palestine Liberation Organization; China to visit my children studying in Beijing; the German Democratic Republic to converse with academic friends; and to Nicaragua, Cuba and Mexico to observe developments in their respective revolutionary movements and to exchange notes with the pertinent leaders.

2. What were your views on the world situation then?

JMS: Even as I was not able to visit the home grounds of the two superpowers, the US and the Soviet Union (except transiting through the Moscow airport) I had a good vantage point over the world situation through exchange of views with political leaders, activists and academic experts knowledgeable about the politics, economics and culture on an international scale.

I was aware of Reagan pushing hard the US advantage in having baited the Soviet Union into an arms race and into its Afghan quagmire to aggravate the deterioration of the Soviet economy, cajoling Gorbachov to speed up capitalist restoration and blame the previous Brezhnev regime for the Soviet economic crisis and corruption and in accommodating China into the world capitalist system by conceding consumer manufacturing. Of course, since the early 1980s, Reagan and Thatcher had already been riding high in promoting neoliberalism to overcome the problem of stagflation plaguing the US economy from the 1970s onwards.

In my conversations with East German acquaintances in 1987-88, they boasted about being more honest and more efficient than the Russians because they were Germans. But I also gained insights from some East German academics at Humboldt University and trade unionists that subtle methods of bureaucratic corruption were taking place, like having poor African countries pay on loan basis for factory products being declared and destined as grants, with the payments flowing to secret private accounts in Swiss banks.

By the time I visited Nicaragua in 1988, the Soviet and East German experts were complaining about the difficulty of helping Nicaragua because of the heavy requirements for lifting the country from the very low level of development left over from the Somoza regime. They talked pretty much like the Gorbachovite writers from the Soviet Academy of Social Sciences complaining about how cheap it was to aid armed revolutions but how costly it was to take on the responsibility for developing underdeveloped countries.

At the same time, in Nicaragua the big compradors were still in control of foreign trade and were bringing in US-made consumer products via Panama and Mexico. Thus they could connive with the US in manipulating supplies and artificial shortages to generate inflation. I had seen the same problem in Indonesia when in the early 1960s the big compradors were colluding with US and Malaysian suppliers in manipulating supplies and scarcities to generate inflation and stir up dissatisfaction against the Sukarno regime.

In China, I observed that the Chinese authorities were pushing hard for the Dengist policy of capitalist reforms and opening up to the world capitalist system. I saw the construction boom and I heard some of my guides criticizing how the economy was getting overheated, with the prices of food supplies going up because of rising demand from the construction workers. They also commented that some of the peasants could build the much-publicized three-story houses because they engaged in some commerce or money-lending or had family members with industrial jobs somewhere else.

In Japan, I saw capitalism at its peak, so to say. The economy and the stock market were thriving. It looked like the Japanese companies were buying up the most prominent real estate assets in the US. But they were using cash from loans collateralized by overvalued real estate assets in Japan. The crisis of overproduction was just being solved by credit abuse and was the prelude to the prolonged crisis and stagnation of a major capitalist country concurrent with the forthcoming collapse of the Soviet Union and revisionist regimes in Eastern Europe.

In India, I observed neoliberalism making its headway at a rapid rate. I saw neoliberalism coming on top of neocolonialism in a semifeudal country. No wonder, I met so many young intellectuals wishing to wage people's war in every city to which I went. I had a chance to converse with the leaders of a wide range of communist parties, especially those of the Communist Party of India (Marxist) and quite a number of Communist Parties adhering to Mao Zedong Thought and the Naxalbari Road of people's war.

In Western Europe, where I was already staying most of the time, I observed the British Labor Party and other social-democratic parties in the European Union veering more and more towards neoliberalism. At first, the pro-worker pretense came disguised as the "third way" between capitalism and socialism or social democracy when in fact the growing bias leaned toward the unbridled capitalist greed of neoliberalism.

3. After the cancellation of your Philippine passport by the Aquino government on September 15, 1988, you were stranded in The Netherlands and you had to apply for political asylum. Whatever happened since then?

JMS: Indeed, I had to apply for political asylum after the cancellation of my passport, which had been calculated by the Aquino regime and the military to force my return to the Philippines and put me in the bag of military personnel waiting at the Manila airport. They seemed not to anticipate that I would apply for asylum. Or else they had wanted me to merely get stranded in The Netherlands.

I applied for political asylum on October 15, 1988. My application cited the severe torture that I had suffered under the Marcos dictatorship and the continuing threat of torture by the same military that had subjected me to physical torture by fist blows and water cure; and even worse to the mental torture of solitary confinement for most of the time that I was under military detention from November 10, 1977 to March 5, 1986.

The Raad van State (Council of State), the highest administrative court in The Netherlands in 1992 recognized me as a political refugee in accordance with the Refugee Convention and ruled that I could not be deported in accordance with the jurisprudence from the Soering case. Thus, I continue to stay in The Netherlands as a recognized refugee protected by the Refugee Convention and Article 3 of the European Convention. I cannot be deported to the Philippines or a third country and put at risk of being deported and subjected to torture in the Philippines.

But after I was put on the EU terrorist list in 2002, the Dutch authorities withdrew all my social benefits, including my living allowance, housing, health insurance, insurance against third party liability and pension. I have been deprived of these even after I won my case before the European Court of Justice for the removal of my name from the EU terrorist list in 2009.

Julie and I have had to find ways of our own in order to subsist and do my research and writing, exercise my freedom of expression and perform duties in the service of the Filipino people, like my being the chief political consultant of the National Democratic Front in peace negotiations with the Manila government.

4. You were able to visit China in 1987 and 1988. Then the mass protests in Tiananmen occurred in Beijing and in other Chinese cities in 1989. Were you taken aback by these events and what caused them?

JMS: When I traveled to China in 1987 and 1988, I noticed many phenomena that could result in mass resistance. The prices of basic commodities were rising steeply because of a number of serious imbalances in the economy. For one, the widespread construction projects were pushing up the demand of construction workers and the urban population for food and other necessities. Besides,agricultural production was experiencing shortfalls, especially because many peasants were being displaced from farming as a result of the dismantling of the communes. The displaced peasants could not find prompt alternative employment in construction and the sweatshops. So they migrated to the cities looking for odd jobs at low wages or roaming the streets like the vagabond gangs in pre-revolutionary China.

When I visited the Beijing University, I noticed that the study and dormitory facilities for the students had not expanded since my earlier visits in the 1960s. The faculty members and students were aghast over the surreptitious removal of the statue of Mao after midnight. I make special mention of Beijing University because many of the demonstrators at Tiananmen in 1989 came from there.

In informal conversations, I learned that the intelligentsia and ordinary people frowned on millionaires becoming members of the Communist Party of China. They were concerned about corruption of government officials in the handling of business licenses and franchises for Chinese and foreign businesses. They resented the growing number of Mercedes Benz and Rolls Royce cars being used by high bureaucrats and their families. Such cars were quite noticeable because at that time swarms of bicycles still occupied the main roads.

Having observed some of the major phenomena, I was not surprised by the mass protests that occurred in 1989 not only in Beijing but also in many other cities of China. The strongest outcry was against inflation and corruption. More people raised the portrait of Mao Zedong and Zhou Enlai to call for revolutionary integrity than those who called for bourgeois democracy and liberalization of everything.

The mass protest at Tiananmen was unnecessarily attacked with brute force on the orders of the Dengist clique. The assault was launched when the mass protest was already subsiding. But the Dengist clique was after the mass intimidation of the Chinese people.

It misrepresented the mass protest as a rebellion against the "socialist order."

5. I remember that the policy of the NDFP up to the collapse of the Soviet Union was to establish friendly relations of anti-imperialist solidarity with the Soviet Union and other East European countries. How did you feel about the outright capitalist restoration in all these countries?

JMS: I was in prison from November 10, 1977 to March 5, 1986. But I came to know later that in the early 1980s, some members of the Central Committee (CC) of the Communist Party of the Philippines (CPP) were disgusted with the revisionist regime and capitalist restoration in China and at the same time were impressed with how much the Soviet Union had helped armed revolutions in Vietnam and in Africa in the 1970s.

Thus the CPP CC adopted the policy of seeking military assistance from the Soviet and pro-Soviet parties, on the political ground of solidarity against US imperialism. The decision stipulated that the National Democratic Front (NDF) take proto-diplomatic or diplomatic steps to approach the aforesaid parties, in the same way that the Palestinian Liberation Organization (PLO) did for the purpose of establishing friendly relations and seeking military assistance.

The CPP could not directly approach the Soviet and pro-Soviet parties because these had recognized the Lavaite revisionist party as their fraternal party in the Philippines. The NDFP spent much effort and expense to approach these revisionist parties. And the net result was only the establishment of relations between the NDF and the National Front of Czechoslovakia in 1989. Soon after that, the Soviet Union and Eastern Europe were in turmoil, the revisionist regimes fell and the Soviet Union no less collapsed.

I felt sorry and sympathetic to the proletariat and people of the Soviet Union and the Eastern European countries that had been betrayed by the modern revisionists, the bourgeois renegades who had grown and gained dominance within the ruling parties of the proletariat. At the same time, I detested the modern revisionism that had been promoted by the Soviet party since 1956 and spread in Eastern Europe and elsewhere.

I have written articles for major publications and given speeches to conferences and seminars against modern revisionism and capitalism that culminated in the years 1989-91. Armando Liwanag's "Stand for Socialism against Modern Revisionism" is the most definitive paper issued by the CPP on the subject.

6. You were a guest of the PLO in its parliamentary session or National Council meeting in 1987 in Algiers. How would you compare the situation of the PLO then and after the collapse of the Soviet Union?

JMS: After being driven out of Beirut, Lebanon in 1982, the PLO transferred its headquarters to Tunis, Tunisia from 1982 to 1991. I think that this was a bleak period in the heroic struggle of the Palestinian people against Israeli Zionism and US imperialism. The PLO became separated from a big Palestinian mass base and was susceptible to unfavorable policies of the Soviet Union, China and certain countries in the Arab League.

As guest, I attended the 18th session of the PLO National Council (legislative body of parliament) in Algiers. The session was characterized by a high sense of unity, militancy and defiance against Israeli Zionism and US imperialism.

The principal achievement of the session was the reunification of the six factions of the PLO which had split over internal disagreements on how to fight Israel. These factions were the Democratic Front for the Liberation of Palestine, the Palestinian Communist Party, the Arab Liberation Front, the Palestinian Liberation Front, the Popular Front for the Liberation of Palestine and Arafat's Al Fatah.

In October 1, 1987, Israel launched an air raid on the PLO headquarters in Tunis. Arafat survived the raid but 60 PLO members including a number of its leaders were killed. In December 1987 the First Intifada started. The Palestinian Uprising consisted of strikes, protest campaigns and stone-throwing by children in Gaza and the West Bank.

The PLO 19th National Council meeting in November 1988 approved the Palestinian Declaration of Independence. The declaration did not explicitly recognize the state of Israel. But an accompanying document refers to the UN Security Council Resolution 242. Then in December, Yasser Arafat made statements that the US interpreted as recognizing Israel in its pre-1967 boundaries.

The declaration failed to refer to Israel as a colonial and occupying power and to define the borders of the Palestinian territory. Nevertheless, the document referred to the historic injustice suffered by the Palestinian Arab people and asserted their right to national self-determination in accordance with the Treaty of Lausanne (1923) and the UN General Assembly Resolution No. 18 in support of the rights of the Palestinians and Palestine. The state of Palestine on Palestinian territory, with its capital Jerusalem, was proclaimed.

Eventually, the PLO National Council called for "multilateral" negotiations on the basis of the UN Security Council Resolution 242. It implied acceptance of the two-state solution and called it a "historic" compromise. This paved the way for the Oslo accords in 1993.

The vulnerabilities of the PLO must be understood in the context of unfavorable events in Jordan, in Lebanon and Syria and in the Arab League. And we should not overlook how Gorbachov was bowing low to Reagan in 1988 and how he met with Bush in 1989 at the Malta Summit in order supposedly to end the Cold War. This was shortly after the fall of the Berlin Wall in 1989. Certainly after the collapse of the Soviet Union in 1991, the PLO and other national liberation movements in the Middle East and Africa had to face a conspicuously changed situation.

7. Between 1987 and 1988 you visited India, the Democratic People's Republic of Korea (DPRK), Nicaragua, Cuba and Mexico. What were your main observations during these visits and what major changes occurred in these countries after 1989?

JMS: In 1987 I observed that the Indian leaders were opening up to the US neoliberal policy and were already adjusting to the dwindling of relations with the Soviet Union, which was already in a severe economic crisis. I had conversations with leaders of the Congress Party and those of various communist parties and all of them were confident of advancing their movements. Several parties adherent to Mao Zedong Thought and the Naxalbari Road were interested in pursuing people's war. The Communist Party of India (People's War) had already started waging people's war.

In the Democratic People's Republic of Korea (DPRK), I had the honor of meeting Comrade Kim Il-Sung who was very supportive of the Filipino people's new democratic revolution under the leadership of the CPP. He was emphatic about self-reliance (Juche) and his resolve to carry out socialist revolution and construction independently of China and the Soviet Union. At the same time, I noticed that the DPRK maintained good relations with its two giant neighbors.

In 1988 I traveled to Nicaragua with an NDF delegation headed by Luis Jalandoni as NDFP Chief International Representative. We noticed how Nicaragua under the Sandinista leadership of Daniel Ortega had to take into account the long-term damage Somoza had wrought to Nicaragua; the economic sanctions, US support for the contras and military threat; and the inadequate support from the Soviet Union and other revisionist-ruled countries in Eastern Europe. After 1988, the US escalated attacks on Nicaragua through the contras and at the same time offered peace negotiations in order to effect regime change in favor of the pro-US oligarchs.

In Cuba, the leaders from the level of Fidel Castro down were already complaining about the limits and defects of economic cooperation with the Soviet Union. They were starting to revive their relations with China in order to gain more space for maneuver. Eventually, Fidel would declare a special period for adjusting to dire circumstances as a result of the disintegration of the revisionist regimes in Eastern Europe and the collapse of the Soviet Union in the years 1989-91.

In Mexico, I had long conversations with leaders of various communist parties and trade union leaders. They expressed hatred for US imperialism and criticized its historical and current interventions in Mexico and in the oppression and exploitation of the Mexican people. The Mexican comrades themselves were unclear about how to start and sustain an armed revolution in Mexico but were helpful to the Guatemalan revolutionaries across the border. At any rate, in the 1990s several armed revolutionary movements in Central America would enter into peace negotiations.

8. After the collapse of the Soviet Union in 1991, the US was beside itself gloating over the fact that it became the sole superpower. The US camp followers—notably academics like Francis Fukuyama et al.—were proclaiming history cannot go beyond capitalism and liberal democracy. How successful was the US in pushing neoliberalism and launching aggressive wars in the former Yugoslavia, Afghanistan, Iraq and so on?

JMS: The US has been quite successful in adopting neoliberalism and imposing it on most of the rest of the world since the early 1980s. The main points in the neoliberal economic policy are the wage freeze, the erosion of social services and worker benefits, the tax cutbacks for capitalists, trade and investment liberalization, privatization of profitable public assets, deregulation of laws and rules that protect, labor, women, children and the environment and the denationalization of the economies of underdeveloped and less developed countries.

The objective of the neoliberal policy is to give all the opportunities to the monopoly capitalists to extract and accumulate monopoly profits on the false presumption that they, not the working people, create the social wealth and generate the jobs. It is a policy for the reign of unbridled greed at the expense of the workers and other working people. But it results in the acceleration of capital accumulation in the hands of the few and brings about faster and ever worsening rounds of the crisis of overproduction.

Using high technology, the monopoly capitalists have been able to accelerate the exploitation of the proletariat and other working people and the concentration of capital so much so that one percent of the world population now possess more wealth than the 99 percent and a mere 26 super-rich persons hold as much wealth as the world population's poorest half or 3.8 billion people.

The capitalist system tries to bounce from every round of economic crisis by abusing credit at the level of the state, corporations and households, thus generating even worse financial crisis. The abuse of credit is an important feature of neoliberalism. Now, the global public debt of close to US$ 250 trillion is the biggest bubble and the biggest problem of the world capitalist system. The bubble may still grow but it will merely protract the occurrence of the sudden burst. This problem is now in the process of exploding despite the futile austerity measures, so-called.

The proletariat and the people of the world have long suffered gravely from the recurrent and worsening rounds of economic and financial crisis. The consequences of neoliberalism involve not only the immense social devastation at the expense of the working people but also the wanton devastation of the environment in the imperialist frenzy to extract natural resources, especially from the underdeveloped countries.

The last big economic and financial crisis that began in 2008 is worse than the crash of 1929 and is still causing global stagnation and depression. It is not being solved but aggravated by the imperialist powers and is leading to another crisis that would be far worse. It would involve the bursting of the public debt bubble and the rampage of cutthroat competition among the imperialist powers as they become more and more protectionist, contrary to the "free" market mantra of neoliberalism. The very life of capitalism is now threatened by capitalism itself.

As in the years of stagflation and the decade of neoliberalism, the interest rates can still be brought down to counter stagnation and be raised to counter inflation. But the public debt will continue to bloat on a rising level of stagflation, which is already coming back with a vengeance beyond the imagination of the monetarists.

The US has also been quite successful in unleashing wars of aggression under its so-called neoconservative policy of expanding its global economic territory by using a full spectrum of soft and hard weapons and taking full advantage of its superiority in high-tech military weaponry. Thus, since the collapse of the Soviet Union, the US has tried to take advantage of its status as sole superpower; and to launch a series of aggressive wars in Yugoslavia, Afghanistan, Iraq, Syria and elsewhere.

These wars have fattened up the US military-industrial complex, with the US economy being made even more lopsided at the expense of socially beneficial civilian production. But the wars of aggression, which appear to be very successful in terms of destruction of lives and property in other countries have not translated into a widely expanded profitable and stable economic territory abroad for the US to exploit.

Under the Nuremberg principles, US imperialism has been the biggest and worst terrorist power by unleashing wars of aggression, such as those in Korea, Vietnam, Afghanistan, the former Yugoslavia, Iraq, Libya, Syria and others. Since the end of World War II, it has slaughtered more than 25 million people and destroyed the social infrastructure of victim countries. Yet, the US has the temerity to adopt the slogan of "anti-terrorism" for justifying its wars of aggression and its promotion of state terrorism on a global scale.

Since the Bush II regime, masterminded or induced the 9/11 incident to override or cover up its questionable electoral victory in 2000, the US has proclaimed a perpetual borderless "war on terror" in order to carry out wars of aggression and step up state terrorism. Together with its puppets and allies, it has earned the ire of the people of the world who adhere to national liberation, democracy and socialism.

9. Since 1989, can you describe the relationship of the US with China as well as with Russia and particularly the one between China and Russia?

JMS: When economic trouble persisted in China after the Tiananmen massacre in 1989, the US in the 1990s poured in more investments into China and loosened up on technology restrictions in order to prop up the capitalist counterrevolution, buoy up the Chinese economy and entice it further to integrate itself into the WTO. The US was glad that from year to year the global economic growth rate remained positive because of China's high growth rate.

But now the US resents the fact that China has maintained a two-tier system of bureaucrat monopoly capitalism and private monopoly capitalism. The state capitalist sector has been using state planning learned from previous socialist experience to achieve Chinese strategic goals, such as raising industrial capacity and producing advanced military weaponry.

The US under Trump wants to upset the Chinese economic rise as a rival in global hegemony. The No. 1 pusher of neoliberalism has now become the chief exponent of protectionism. It is also dazed by the simultaneous growth of high-tech military technology in the hands of both China and Russia and is thrashing the US-Russian pact on the nonproliferation of the nuclear weapons.

The collapse of the Soviet Union gave way to the rise of Russian imperialism with high-tech military prowess and with oil and gas resources that Germany and other EU countries need. The US reacts to these facts by pushing the expansion of the NATO to Eastern Europe and making provocations on the borders of Russia, especially in Ukraine and Poland, with offers to Europe of shale gas and the further discovery and development of energy resources in the North Sea.

The Trump regime has been posing as even more belligerent than its predecessors towards Russia, notwithstanding evidence or indications that Trump's electoral campaign had been supported by Russia. Trump has withdrawn the US from the nuclear nonproliferation treaty with Russia and other countries.

Meanwhile, Putin has reminded Trump that Russia possesses the military capability to wipe out both the US and Western Europe in thirty minutes. Trump's bellicose posturing can be neutralized in the same manner that Kim Jong-Un has done with firmness and diplomatic skills, outmaneuvering Trump by strengthening efforts at reunification with the Republic of Korea and getting the support of China.

China has been collaborating with Russia to build the Eurasian economy, undermine the US dominance in the IMF, World Bank and WTO with the Brazil-Russia-India-China-South Africa (BRICS) group and its Development Bank and to counter the military expansion of the US and NATO through the Shanghai Cooperation Organization (SCO). It has undertaken the Belt and Road Initiative (BRI) to link up the widest economic and trade relations mainly through railways, roads, bridges and sea ports to surpass the previous maritime superiority of the Western powers since the 16th century.

Since the financial meltdown of 2008, which has resulted in a prolonged depression and stagnation of the world economy, the US has gone into an accelerated strategic decline, especially in economic terms. The increase in the number of imperialist powers, with the entry of China and Russia, puts the US in a multilateral world, in which it cannot dictate its wishes as easily as before.

The balance of strength among the imperialist powers is changing. And the US response to the challenge is to turn to protectionism and further belligerence, thus intensifying inter-imperialist contradictions and aggravating the crisis of the world capitalist system.

The intensifying competition and political rivalry among the imperialist powers can result in greater exploitation of the proletariat and people of the world and in the growing danger of inter-imperialist wars. But to avoid inter-imperialist war and mutual destruction with the use of nuclear weapons, the imperialist powers can collude to keep passing the burden of the crisis to the oppressed peoples and nations and ravaging their human and natural resources.

The proletariat and people in the underdeveloped countries are driven to wage resistance against the increased exploitation and oppression and to fight for national and social liberation. And the proletariat and people in the imperialist countries shoulder the special duty of winning the battle for democracy and socialism and disabling and thereby preventing the monopoly bourgeoisie from destroying humankind with either nuclear weapons or global warming as a result of monopoly capitalist firms ruining the environment.

10. While having stayed so long in The Netherlands, what changes have you observed in Western Europe since 1989? How would you define the relationship between EU vis-à-vis Russia and China then and now?

JMS: In the years from 1989 to 1991, the monopoly bourgeoisie of Western Europe was as gleeful as the US over the socioeconomic and political turmoil in China, the Soviet Union and Eastern Europe, especially over the fall of the Berlin Wall and the collapse of the Soviet Union. The European Union stood solid as a bulwark of monopoly capitalism against socialism.

The EU has always tended to go along with the US in relation to Russia, despite complaints of certain countries, like Germany, France and Italy, over the unilateral actions of the US that are quite horrible and difficult to support. The EU has followed the lead of the US in supporting the "color revolutions" in countries neighboring Russia, the neofascists in Ukraine, the violent attacks on the Russians in the Donetsk and Lugansk regions and the sanctions against Russia.

Germany is one country that sometimes takes exception to the most offensive acts of the US against Russia. It has a huge industrial system that is in constant need of the oil and gas from Russia. But any conservative leadership in Germany easily bends to the US wishes on grounds of seeking to improve political and economic conditions in favor of the US and West European investments and other interests.

With regard to China, EU seems to be more friendly to it than to Russia in the absence of any direct bone of contention. But in general, taking into account issues in the Asia-Pacific region and other global regions, the EU also tends to side with the US. The Atlantic Alliance may at times be shaky but there are still more things that bind the US and EU than those that strain them.

The current status of the inter-imperialist contradictions shows the alignment of the traditional imperialist powers (US, EU and Japan) against the new imperialist powers (China and Russia). At the same time, there are contradictions among countries within the same blocs because it is in the nature of any imperialist power to put one over the other whenever necessary to maximize profits or overcome crisis.

11. In what ways have the US and China cooperated and contended with each other in economic and political terms?

JMS: The US and China have been the biggest and main partners in the global propagation and implementation of the neoliberal policy until Trump became president and raised certain major objections to

Chinese economic policy. At critical junctions in the advance of capitalism in China, the US has been assisting China.

The US immediately welcomed the overthrow of the proletariat and the reversal of the Maoist line in 1976, the 1978 capitalist reforms and opening up to the capitalist world and the reinforcement of Chinese capitalism after the Tiananmen massacre of 1989. All the while the US has pressed China to come fully to the fold of the World Trade Organization and to dissolve its state-owned enterprises.

The economic rise of China owes much to US trade, investment and technological accommodation. A key to China's success story is the long-running export surpluses in trade with the biggest consumer market of the world and the inevitable flow of US investments and new technology in the operation of sweatshops and the sale of new equipment to China from the US and its traditional allies.

Now, here comes Trump expressing resentment over the Made-in-China 2025 plan, the development of major industries under the state banks and state-owned enterprises and the production of high-tech military weapons, even improving on those acquired from the US and its allies before the US and EU imposed their arms embargo on China after the Tiananmen incident in 1989. Trump wants to take protectionist measures against China, keep US investments at home to revive consumer manufacturing and prevent China's technological advance. He has gone so far as to call off the Trans-Pacific Partnership Agreement (TPPA).

It was only quite recently that the US began taking action to take back its previous accommodations to China and to foul up China's economic rise. In previous times, the US had stressed more its political rather than economic differences with China over policies related to the US wars of aggression, military interventions and blockades against third parties. The US has been sensitive to China's alliance with Russia on political issues.

12. What do you think of the shifts of US policy from Bush, Jr. through Obama to Trump as regards the Asia-Pacific region in the 21st century? What roles are Japan and Europe currently playing in the major contradictions between the US and China?

JMS: In general, Obama wanted to maintain economic partnership with China. He seemed to understand the mutual benefit for China and the US in letting the former enjoy its huge annual export surpluses. He was already alarmed by the advance of Chinese military technology and the conspicuously increased deployment of Chinese air and naval power. Thus, he declared the policy of a strategic pivot of 60 percent of US air and naval assets to East Asia to contain China's military threat.

In the case of Trump, he has junked the Trans-Pacific Partnership Agreement (TPPA) out of fear that it would include China eventually. And he has taken a protectionist stand against China and has proceeded to impose steep tariffs on China's exports to the US. He has undertaken actions against major Chinese IT firms. He is bent on further measures against China under his slogan of Made in the US and Make America Great Again.

In Northeast Asia, the US is siding with Japan in accordance with the US-Japan Mutual Defense Treaty against China over the islands captured by Japan in World War II. In Southeast Asia, the US aligns itself with countries opposed to the claims of China over 90 percent of the South China Sea. The Philippines and other Southeast Asian countries base themselves on the UN Convention on the Law of the Sea (UNCLOS). In fact the Philippines has won the case against China before the Permanent Court of Arbitration in The Hague in 2016.

Japan and Western Europe have allied themselves with the US in its major contradictions with China. At the same time, they look after their own interests and maintain a nuanced policy towards China. The US is deliberately encouraging Japan to stand up to China not only because of the Chinese islands occupied by Japan but also because it has been a long-time US partner in exploiting cheap labor and natural resources in Southeast Asian countries. But Japan, which China has displaced in manufacturing, is now more interested in selling to and investing in China where many Japanese conglomerates make 25 percent of their profits.

The EU tends to side with the US within the context of the traditional Atlantic Alliance and the alignment of the traditional powers against new imperialist powers. At the same time, the EU and particular EU countries will look for ways to benefit and protect their respective national interests distinct from US wishes and the alliance of traditional imperialist powers.

13. In the EU there are now strong centrifugal tendencies with the rise among others of Eurosceptic political parties and movements. How is this a factor in the EU's relationship with the US, Russia and

China? How should progressive and revolutionary forces regard this development?

JMS: Because of the worsening crisis of the world capitalist system, there is a growing tendency of the neoliberal alliance of imperialist powers to disintegrate. Most conspicuous is the US under Trump becoming protectionist vis a vis China, contravening its old long-running role of using the slogan of free trade to dominate less developed countries.

Most conspicuous in Europe is Germany striving to access the cheapest energy supply for its huge industrial capacity and is availing of the Russian supply of gas independently of US dictates. Even NATO member Turkey is defying the US as it allows the stream of Russian gas through its borders and its purchase of S-400 Missile System. By these and other indications, the centrifugal tendencies are rising among political parties and movements in Europe and thereabouts.

My point is that the increasingly conspicuous sight of the imperialist powers acting in contradiction with each other results in nationalist currents among the bourgeois politicians, parties and their constituencies. The old anti-communist line against the Soviet Union and China during the Cold War that generated the NATO, European Union and the Euro-US Atlantic alliance is dead. China and Russia have joined the ranks of the imperialist powers and are increasingly competing with the US and are playing for advantages in relations with the EU or particular EU member-countries.

The nationalist currents generated by contradictions among imperialist states in Europe also tend to combine with people's grievances over the exploitative and oppressive consequences of neoliberalism and the costs of aggressive wars in arousing and generating scepticism over as well as outright opposition to the EU and the US-Euro Atlantic alliance.

Thus, we see the phenomena of Brexit and similar tendencies in particular EU member-countries and the rise of populist movements of either the progressive kind, like the Yellow Vest Movement in France, that hold to account the bourgeois politicians in power for raising regressive taxes and imposing austerity measures; or the fascist kind that blames immigrants and the EU laws that protect the migrant workers and refugees for the escalating conditions of exploitation and oppression since the financial meltdown of 2007-2008.

The progressive and revolutionary forces should recognize the growing inter-imperialist contradictions and the rise of populist movements of the reactionary or progressive kind under conditions in which the revolutionary parties of the proletariat are still weak and are blocked by neoliberal, social democratic, vestigial revisionist and petty bourgeois liberal forces and currents.

The revolutionary forces should recognize that with firmness in principle, flexibility in policy, militancy and perseverance they can take advantage of the inter-imperialist crisis and rise of populist movements in order to build their own strength and their united front with the progressive anti-imperialist forces.

Chapter II

Impact of global changes on the Philippines

1. What is the impact of the restoration of capitalism in former socialist countries on the Philippines and the Filipino people in general and the CPP and the revolutionary movement in particular?

JMS: The Philippines and the Filipino people are dominated by a semicolonial and semifeudal system servile to US imperialism. They have long been subject to pro-imperialist propaganda since the US conquest of the country in the early years of the 20th century, to anti-Bolshevik propaganda since the 1917 victory of the Great October Socialist Revolution and to the anti-communist propaganda during the Cold War after World War II.

The exploiting classes and their political agents have used the state, reactionary nonstate institutions, political parties, mass media and educational media to echo the triumphalist line of the US that socialism is dead and capitalism is forever as a result of the restoration of capitalism in the former socialist countries.

Most vulnerable to the influence of the reactionary classes and their agents are the politically backward and middle sections of the broad masses. But there is already a growing politically advanced section of the masses under the leadership and influence of the Communist Party of the Philippines, the revolutionary forces and the legal mass organizations of the national democratic movement.

Since the early 1960s, the CPP and the revolutionary movement of the people have understood and exposed the phenomenon of modern revisionism and the actual process of restoring capitalism, which started in the Soviet Union in 1956. Since their break from the Lava revisionist party in 1966, the proletarian revolutionaries who established the CPP in 1968 have been well versed on the ideological dispute between the Soviet party and the Chinese party and have put forward the anti-revisionist line in the CPP's First Great Rectification Movement.

They have extended their anti-revisionist line to an understanding of Soviet modern revisionism as having caught up with the Chinese revolution through the Chinese students and experts and worker-trainees in the Soviet Union in the 1950s. The great Mao and the Chinese

Communist Party under his leadership had to struggle against the influence of Soviet modern revisionism and against the Chinese modern revisionists and capitalist-roaders who opposed the Great Leap Forward, the Socialist Education Movement and the Great Proletarian Cultural Revolution.

The restoration of capitalism in former socialist countries, including China, has proven to the CPP and the revolutionary movement that modern revisionism, if not effectively combated and defeated, can lead to the undermining of socialism and the overthrow of the working class. Thus, the CPP puts the highest value to Mao's theory and practice of continuing revolution under proletarian dictatorship in order to combat revisionism, prevent the restoration of capitalism and consolidate socialism.

2. What has been the CPP's explanation of the phenomenon of modern revisionism and the restoration of capitalism?

JMS: The most comprehensive and profound explanation of the phenomenon of revisionism by the CPP is put forward by Armando Liwanag in "Stand for Socialism against Modern Revisionism." Modern revisionism is traced to the waning of the proletarian class stand within the Communist Party and among the intelligentsia and bureaucracy upon the success of the socialist construction and the expansion of the educational system.

It was after the success of the first five-year economic plan in the Soviet Union that Stalin introduced the erroneous line in the 1936 Soviet Constitution that there were no more classes and class struggle in Soviet society, except the struggle between the Soviet people and the imperialist enemy. He obfuscated the continuing existence of classes and class struggle, which led to a failure to distinguish and correctly handle the contradictions among the people and those between the people and the enemy.

At first, the petty bourgeois mode of thinking arose and spread among the new intelligentsia and bureaucracy in the ruling party, economy and various institutions. They presumed that building socialism was merely a matter of raising production and applying science and technology without bothering about the proletarian class stand. In due course, the new bourgeoisie became a reality bred by the selfish impulses of the intelligentsia and bureaucrats, the acquisition of privileges and the influence of the international bourgeoisie.

Before his death, Stalin realized his error in thinking that classes and class struggle had ceased to exist in the Soviet Union. He became aware that the Party and the government bureaucracy and other institutions were already swamped by bourgeois-minded personnel. But it was too late for him to make any rectification.

In 1956 Khrushchov denounced the "personality cult" of Stalin and held him responsible for crimes, which were the result of the incorrect handling of class contradictions; i.e., misconstruing or misjudging non-hostile contradictions among the people as hostile contradictions between the enemy and the people." But the anti-Stalin attack was also a cover for pushing the modern revisionist line and restoring capitalism by decentralizing the economic ministries, fracturing the socialist economy and autonomizing industrial enterprises and agricultural collectives and putting them on an individualized cost-and-profit basis and giving the managers hire-and-fire power over the workers. He also initiated the opening of the "free market" in agriculture to free up and open the door wide for the reemergence of the rich peasants or kulaks and the rise of merchants.

After he replaced Khrushchov, Brezhnev recentralized the economic ministries and enterprises previously decentralized by his predecessor. He did so to facilitate the centralization of resources for the benefit of the central bureaucracy and for the arms race. But he did something even bigger than Khrushchov by way of restoring capitalism. He allowed the corrupt monopoly bureaucrats and their private collaborators to form Mafia-type syndicates to misdeclare and steal the products of the state-owned enterprises and sell these in the expanded "free market."

The Soviet economy deteriorated tremendously due to corruption, the arms race, the war of aggression in Afghanistan and other adventures. By the time Gorbachov came to power, he could use the ghost of Brezhnev as a whipping boy and decry the inefficiency of monopoly bureaucrat capitalism in order to push the privatization of state enterprises and the full restoration of capitalism.

I think that Soviet modern revisionism seeped into the ranks of the Chinese communist cadres during the time of Khrushchov when he was able to promote revisionism also in Eastern Europe. The worship of anything Soviet, even if revisionist, was promoted by quite a number of Chinese students, experts and worker-trainees who had gone to the Soviet Union for study and training, very much the same way that Chinese students went to the US in even far larger numbers after Deng was able to enforce capitalist reforms and opening up to the capitalist world.

In China, modern revisionists and capitalist-roaders like Liu Shaoqi and Deng Xiaoping dished out the line that classes and class struggle were dying out and that the most intense class struggle had ended. This was the line that gave so much problem to Mao and the proletarian revolutionaries. Thus, they had to state categorically that classes and class struggle continued to exist and class struggle is the key link to the advance of socialist revolution and construction.

Mao put forward the theory and practice of continuing revolution under proletarian dictatorship through the Great Proletarian Cultural Revolution in order to combat revisionism, prevent capitalist restoration and consolidate socialism. From 1966 to 1976, the GPCR appeared to be successful through twists and turns. But after Mao's death, Deng was able to defeat it through a coup and thus open the way to the full-scale capitalist restoration.

3. Was the CPP ever adversely affected by the ideological US offensive line that the socialist cause is dead, that history cannot go beyond capitalism and liberal democracy and that national liberation movements are passé and futile in view of neoliberal globalization?

JMS: As a whole, the CPP central leadership and the general membership were not adversely affected by the US offensive line that the socialist cause is dead and that even the national liberation movements are passé in view of neoliberal globalization coming on top of neocolonialism.

Only a handful of unremolded and unstable petty-bourgeois elements who had crept into the CPP were so overwhelmed by the rapid and full restoration of capitalism in revisionist-ruled countries that they even thought that the national liberation movements had become passé and could not hold their ground against neoliberal globalization.

They went to the extent of praising Fidel Ramos for waving the flag of neoliberalism in the 1990s. They privatized their foreign-funded NGOs and at the same time sought jobs from the Ramos regime after helping in the failed electoral campaign of Jovito Salonga. They had more success in joining the succeeding Estrada, Arroyo and Aquino II regimes. They rationalized their renegacy by prating that the masses were tired of armed revolution.

The CPP has been outstanding in upholding the new democratic revolution with a socialist perspective and in combating the US-instigated neoliberal policy of imperialist globalization. I am proud to have written so much on these subjects and contributed to the resoluteness and militancy of the CPP and the revolutionary movement of the people in exposing and rejecting the policy.

No imperialist force or local reactionary force can use any ideological or political offensive to invalidate Marxism-Leninism-Maoism and the general line of people's democratic revolution, which is well-grounded on Philippine history and current circumstances, and is in accordance with the urgent demands of the people for national liberation and democracy against US imperialism and the semicolonial and semifeudal ruling system.

Even during the years from 1989 to 1991, it was clear to the CPP cadres and members that the crisis in the revisionist-ruled countries was part of the general crisis of global capitalism. Even a traditional capitalist power, Japan, was in serious economic crisis as a result of the crisis of overproduction and abuse of credit. Since then, the crisis of global capitalism has become more frequent and worse leading up to the economic and financial crisis of 2008, which is still running but is already being overtaken by a looming worse crisis threatening the very life of the world capitalist system.

4. China had been engaged in capitalist reforms and has integrated itself into the world capitalist system since 1978. But it has retained the Red flag and the Chinese communist party as the ruling Party. Has this ambiguous posture of China not confused the CPP?

JMS: Because of its adherence to the teachings of Mao, the CPP has never been confused by the actual accelerated restoration of capitalism under the Dengist policy of dismantling the communes, capitalist reforms and opening up to the capitalist world and the simultaneous masquerade of retaining the name of the Chinese Communist Party as ruling party and waving the Red flag.

The CPP has always been critical of modern revisionism and capitalist restoration in China that prevailed after the death of Mao in 1976 and has regarded its relations with the CPC as no longer based on a comradely Marxist-Leninist basis but rather on the friendly basis of solidarity until the CPC itself decided to cut off all relations with the CPP in 1989.

The CPP has long scorned such Chinese assertions that its capitalist restoration is still socialism with Chinese characteristics, that capitalist reforms are socialist ones, that opening up to the capitalist world is freedom from the supposed narrowness of proletarian internationalism and that socialism and communism are but vehicles of collective irresponsibility in which the people are entitled to the common pot even if they do not work.

China has become a full-fledged capitalist country and has become an imperialist power, partaking of the economic features of imperialism defined by Lenin. With regard to the fifth feature, which is the completion of the global spread of capitalism and the consequent struggle for a redivision of the world among the imperialist powers, the Philippines is directly on the path of Chinese expansionism in terms of deployment of surplus capital and the use of military prowess to violate Philippine sovereign rights in the West Philippine Sea.

With the traitorous complicity of the Duterte regime, China is now trying to make the Philippines its debt colony by burdening it with high interest loans for overpriced infrastructure projects carried out by Chinese, instead of Filipino contractors and workers. Duterte's treasonous complicity has extended to allowing China to take over features of the West Philippine Sea in violation of the sovereign rights of the Philippines under the UN Convention on the Law of the Sea (UNCLOS) and in contempt of the legal victory of the Philippines against China in the case decided by the Permanent Court of Arbitration in The Hague in 2016.

5. How does the CPP react to China's stopping both the moral and material assistance to revolutionary movements in Southeast Asia, including the Philippines, in accordance with the line of peace, stability and development?

JMS: The CPP takes the view that Dengist China adopted the line of pursuing "peace and development" in Southeast Asia and sought to liquidate armed revolutionary movements in the region, especially since the late 1970s. Even while Mao was alive, China's foreign policy was to normalize relations with the US and avoid any action that would counter this in line with China's opposition to Soviet social-imperialism and the deployment of one million Soviet troops on the Sino-Soviet border.

At first, China continued to support the Khmer Rouge and went to the extent of ordering the Chinese army to cross the border with Vietnam in 1978 to punish the Vietnamese for invading Cambodia. Then, in consideration of Thailand's toleration of the cross-border camps of the Khmer Rouge, China accommodated Thailand by cutting off support to the Thai Communist Party and causing the closure of the radio broadcast station based in the Chinese-Thai border and shared by Southeast Asian parties.

The Central Committee delegations of Southeast Asian parties based in Beijing had been paralyzed as they were relocated outside Beijing and then later allowed to return to Beijing only to be pressured in the early 1980s to seek ways of leaving China. The delegations were taken to task by the CPC general secretary Hu Yaobang for siding with the GPCR. The central leadership of the Burmese Communist Party was cut off from its army in Burma. Also, the exiled leadership of the Malayan Communist Party was induced to leave China after Malaysia offered to normalize relations with China.

In the case of the CPP, it ceased to expect any assistance from China in 1974 because of the difficulties in receiving assistance from across the sea to the archipelago and because of the policy of China to avoid displeasing the US. The CPP CC delegation to China became paralyzed when it was relocated to Hunan province. Later on, like the PKI CC delegation, it was advised to seek ways for its members to leave China in the early 1980s.

It is a blessing in disguise that the CPP did not receive any substantial material assistance from China comparable to that given to Vietnam and Cambodia. It has learned to be self-reliant in developing people's war against the US-propped ruling system. Thus, it has lasted for more than 50 years and is still growing in strength by relying on the masses and seizing weapons from the enemy.

When the Khmer Rouge was left as the only armed movement active in the Southeast Asian mainland, China encouraged it to go into a series of peace negotiations with the government in Phnom Penh under UN auspices. The Khmer Rouge accepted being ultimately confined to a so-called peace zone until it took a final dive into self-disintegration and self-destruction.

6. After the collapse of the Soviet Union in 1991, the US was in an even better position to push its neoliberal economic policy throughout the world, especially with the Chinese economy in tow. How has the Philippines been affected by the so-called neoliberal globalization?

JMS: Even before the collapse of the Soviet Union, the US had begun to impose the neoliberal policy on the Philippines in certain ways. After Marcos received so much concessional loans from the World Bank before the neoliberal policy regime or still under the neo-Keynesian times, the US and the world capitalist system started to tighten credit and put the Marcos regime in a bind from 1979 onwards, with the increased interest rates on loans. The construction firms of the Marcos cronies were redirected to the Middle East oil-producing countries.

It was after the downfall of Marcos in 1986 when the US required the Aquino regime to liberalize trade but the increased interest rates on the accumulated Marcos-incurred foreign debt restrained it from taking more substantial foreign loans. The Aquino regime therefore had to resort to heavy local borrowing.

It was during the presidency of Ramos that the US was able to bring the neoliberal policy into full play in the Philippines. The Ramos regime was compelled to liberalize trade and investments in favor of the US and other foreign monopoly firms, privatize state-owned prime land and government corporations and carry out deregulation.

In return, the Ramos regime was provided loans, especially from Japan, for a boom in private construction and for covering trade and budgetary deficits. The Philippine economy looked prosperous with a growing GDP bloated by import-dependent consumption, increased government spending and nonindustrial investments until the Asian financial crisis of 1997 hit the Philippines hard.

The Philippine economy was in the doldrums during the short presidency of Estrada who was forced to resign by mass protest actions because of corruption and the deterioration of the economy. His successor Arroyo benefited as the region recovered from the Asian financial crisis, with China making new orders for semiconductors after taking advantage of the drastic dive of the so-called Southeast Asian tigers.

The Aquino II regime was favored by the heavy flow of hot money or portfolio investments of the US hedge funds in pursuit of profit, which was higher in the Philippines than in the US. The hot money served to bloat the GDP from 2010 to 2013 but went mainly into the stock market and money market and not into putting up any productive enterprise.

The portfolio investments started to flow out of the Philippines in 2014 upon the steady rise in US interest rates.

The current Duterte regime is in bad shape economically and financially. The persistent neoliberal policy has made the economy more lopsided than ever before, with the exploiting classes having most of the wealth and income and further impoverishing the working people. Unemployment and mass poverty have worsened to unprecedented levels. Remittances of overseas contract workers have stagnated because of the prolonged global depression since 2008. Foreign direct investments and foreign loans have decreased.

Even the high-interest loans for overpriced infrastructure projects have come to the Philippines not as fast as Duterte has hoped for because China is pressing for more gains in the West Philippine Sea, not only the acquiescence to the Chinese-made islands (there are now seven, all militarized) but also a joint exploration and development agreement that would put China in control of the offshore oil and gas resources estimated to be worth US$ 60 trillion. In this regard, Duterte is being exposed as a traitor and paid agent of China despite his continuing puppetry to US imperialism$ 60 trillion.

7. In what ways has the US used the 9-11 events and the ever escalating war on terror in order to aggrandize itself in the Philippines as well as in the entire Asia-Pacific region?

JMS: Certainly the US has used the 9-11 events and the so-called war on terror to aggrandize itself in the Philippines, Southeast Asia and the entire Asia-Pacific region. Soon after 9/11, it extended the "war" to the Philippines and described the country as the "second front." Thus, Oplan Enduring Freedom-Philippines was imposed on the Philippines in January 2002 against the supposed Islamic terrorist groups like Abu Sayyaf and Jemaah Islamiyah. Arroyo welcomed the operational plan.

The UN Special Operations Command-Pacific deployed military personnel to advise and assist the reactionary armed forces of the Philippines. It augmented the rotating US military forces under the Visiting Forces Agreement. The "war on terror" in the Philippines subsequently assumed different names, like Operation Smiles and PACOM Augmentation Team. The latest name is Operation Pacific Eagle as of 2018.

The "war on terror" is just one more US excuse for maintaining its military presence in the Philippines. It circumvents the congressional oversight of military assistance in connection with human rights. Ironically, the major target Abu Sayyaf was actually created by the US Central Intelligence Agency (CIA) and the Armed Forces of the Philippines (AFP) intelligence officers to contest and weaken the influence of the Moro National Liberation Front in Basilan and Sulu in the 1990s. The CIA creation of Abu Sayyaf long preceded the creation of the Islamic State in the Middle East in recent times.

The extension of the US "war on terror" to the Bangsamoro areas in Mindanao puts US military power in a vantage position of securing energy and other precious natural resources while entrenching itself at the geographic center of Islamic Southeast Asia. Together, the Philippines, Indonesia and Malaysia comprise a major hub of the Asia-Pacific region.

8. What is the impact of the US overthrow of the Ghaddafi government on the Bangsamoro movement for self-determination, particularly on the Moro National Liberation Front, whose leadership—notably chairman Nur Misuari—resided in Libya for quite some time?

JMS: The Bangsamoro movement most affected by the US-NATO overthrow of the Ghaddafi government is the Moro National Liberation Front, which received assistance from Libya for a long time from the 1970s. Ghaddafi lessened support to the MNLF since the 1990s while he tried to be prudent and friendly to the US and the NATO in order to fend off sanctions.

However, since 1993, the MNLF was able to work out a peace agreement with the Ramos regime under the auspices of the Organization of Islamic Countries (OIC). The Manila government allowed the MNLF to govern the Autonomous Region in Muslim Mindanao (ARMM) and to get budgetary support and other resources.

It is another long story away from your question how the MNLF fared in governing ARMM. It was during the term of Arroyo that the MNLF split and the Sulu-based Misuari leadership was accused of corruption and incompetence. The anti-Misuari faction based in Maguindanao prevailed in the ARMM. But eventually the ARMM fell under the rule of the Ampatuan dynasty, which was scandalously corrupt and murderous and gained notoriety for herding and murdering a big number of journalists and other people in 2009.

9. With the support of the Islamic countries to the Bangsamoro movements apparently weakened, have the US and Manila governments gained the upper hand and can they now apply the so-called war on terror to suppress any Moro resistance movement for self-determination?

JMS: Of course, the Manila government has been taking advantage of the weakening support of the Islamic countries to the Bangsamoro movements. It uses diplomatic actions and the support of the US to paralyze and frustrate the support of Islamic countries to the Bangsamoro. At the same time, it uses a two-handed policy against the Bangsamoro people's struggle for self-determination and democracy.

With one hand, it executes whatever is the current strategic military plan to suppress the Bangsamoro movements and invoke the "war on terror." Duterte has imposed martial law in Mindanao both against the NPA and the Bangsamoro rebels since May 2017. With another hand, it tries to arrange agreements of compromise with the strongest Bangsamoro movements like the MNLF and the Moro Islamic Liberation Front (MILF).

In view of the split and weakening of the MNLF, the Manila government has been giving more attention to arranging a peace agreement with the MILF. It exploits the contradictions between the MILF and the MNLF and their respective internal weaknesses to carry out a divide-and-rule strategy at the expense of the Moro people and in favor of the traditional ruling dynasties which are inclined to collaborate with the Manila government.

10. Will the final approval of the Bangsamoro Organic Law (BOL) and the subsequent formation of BARRM have an adverse effect on the Filipino people's struggle for national and social liberation? For instance, more military forces will be deployed for suppressing any progressive movement.

JMS: The ratification and implementation of the Bangsamoro Organic Law (BOL) will certainly please the MILF and its constituency the most because the MILF assumes the leadership of the Bangsamoro Transition Authority (BTA) of the Bangsamoro Autonomous Region in Muslim Mindanao (BARMM). But several movements and groups are ready to continue armed resistance in areas where the MILF ceased to fight.

The MILF can try its best to engage and accommodate the MNLF factions of Misuari and Mus Sema. But the Misuari faction will be more difficult to persuade to come on board the BTA. And there are also other groups like the Bangsamoro Islamic Freedom Fighters, the Abu Sayyaf groups of Basilan and Sulu and the Maute group. Moreover, the Maranaos detest the Duterte regime for the destruction of Marawi City and the prolonged evacuation and dislocation of its inhabitants.

The situation in Bangsamoro will continue to be complex, volatile and violent because of the scheme of the Manila government to use the MILF to suppress any rebellious movements or groups. The reactionary armed forces and national police will continue to deploy a large number of personnel in the Bangsamoro part of Mindanao, thus reducing the amount of troops to deploy against the NPA.

The revolutionary forces of the Filipino people's struggle for national and social liberation are growing in strength in the greater part of Mindanao and the rest of the Philippines, irrespective of developments in the relationship of the Manila government with any of the major Bangsamoro mass movements. In areas where the armed personnel of any of the Bangsamoro movements or groups have ceased to operate, the Moro masses are seeking to link-up with and join the NPA and participate in the national democratic movement in the hope of advancing their right to self-determination.

11. The revolutionary underground/movement has followed very early on in its history a policy of decentralized operations and this has contributed in no small way to it's survival and growth during the Marcos dictatorship. But do you think this has also given rise to a problem of "localism" that may have contributed to such problems as "conservatism," among others?

JMS: In the people's war in the Philippines, the policy of decentralized operations is subordinate to the line of centralized leadership in ideology and politics. The centralized and decentralized aspects are complementary and interactive. They are in harmony with the principle of democratic centralism within the Communist Party of the Philippines.

Since the beginning of the armed revolution in 1969, the CPP has been cognizant of the need to expand the New People's Army in as many new areas as possible in order to preclude the enemy from destroying the first guerrilla front that we established in the second district of Tarlac by simply concentrating on it. Thus, we trained immediately cadres for the regions of Cagayan Valley, Ilocos and Cordillera, Southern Tagalog and Western Visayas.

The first expansion teams dispatched to different regions and subsequent teams to more regions within the next five to ten years were highly conscious of the line of centralized leadership in ideology and politics and the policy of decentralized relations in consonance with the Party's principle of democratic centralism and the command structure of the New People's Army from the national level to the lower levels.

To preempt the problem of localism and to cure real cases of localism, the CPP ensures the continuous flow of cadres from the central level to the lower levels, calls for lower cadres to attend study sessions and politico-military training at a higher level, redeploys cadres from one locality to another, and promotes lower level cadres to a higher level. Most important of all, CPP cadres and NPA commanders and fighters are imbued with the just cause of achieving the people's democratic revolution throughout the Philippines and with the spirit of proletarian internationalism.

The problem of conservatism may be intertwined with the problems of localism and so-called civilianization. Basically the problem of conservatism consists of overconcentrating on mass work, overdispersing small units of the NPA and neglecting to plan and launch tactical offensives in order to increase the arms and formations of the NPA. The interrelated problems of conservatism, localism, civilianization, and overdispersal of small NPA units are being solved by the strategic decision of the CPP to intensify the armed struggle and redeploy the NPA units accordingly.

The NPA can launch tactical offensives against the weak points of the enemy and win victories because its forces are spread nationwide and deeply rooted among the toiling masses of workers and peasants more than ever before. More experienced and effective NPA commanders and fighters are being redeployed from stronger guerrilla fronts to weaker guerrilla fronts in order to raise the general level of development of the NPA and the people's war.

12. What are the subjective factors and objective conditions in the Philippines that will most likely be in favor to your struggle, irrespective of the external factors and conditions?

JMS: The objective conditions favorable to the Philippine revolution arise mainly from the worsening chronic crisis of the semicolonial and semifeudal ruling system. The result is the escalating oppression and exploitation of the people. The worsening conditions of oppression and exploitation drive the people to undertake the various forms of resistance, especially armed struggle.

The subjective factors most important in the revolutionary struggle are the CPP, which is the party of the working class leading the revolution, the NPA and its auxiliary forces (people's militia and self-defense units), the NDFP, the mass organizations of various classes and sectors, the alliances of various types and scales and the local organs of political power, which constitute the people's democratic government.

13. Is the Philippine revolutionary movement receiving any material assistance from abroad? If "yes," what is its proportion in relation to the resources produced by self-reliance?

JMS: The Philippine revolutionary movement does not receive any military assistance from abroad. Neither does it receive any material assistance beyond what parties, organizations and movements are capable of extending as tokens of solidarity. The moral and political support is incalculably far greater than such material tokens.

The Philippine revolutionary movement relies mainly on the membership dues, productive work and donations. The people's democratic government is responsible for tax collection to defray the costs of general administration, public education, mass organizing, land reform, raising production, health and sanitation, self-defense, arbitration and justice, cultural work, disaster relief and protection of the environment.

Based on my reading and some well-informed articles, more than 95 percent of the arms in the hands of the people's army, people's militia and self-defense forces have been seized from the enemy in military operations. The rest come from donors and local purchases. All previous attempts of the revolutionary movement to receive military assistance have been unsuccessful.

The enemy in the Philippines is still the best source of weapons for the revolutionary forces of the Filipino people. It is the most efficient transport and supply officer of the NPA. It deploys armed personnel on a wide scale. And the NPA simply chooses the enemy weak points to hit in an ambush or raid in order to seize the arms.

☆ ☆ ☆

Chapter III

Working against the tide to uphold revolution

1. In the aftermath of the upheavals which restored capitalism in former socialist countries, what studies and actions did you personally undertake?

JMS: I did a lot of reading and research, which covered reading materials from academic and research centers, news agencies, and the contending political parties and leading figures. There were reading materials from China, the former Soviet Union and Eastern Europe and of course from the traditional capitalist countries.

I had to augment the information about modern revisionism and the steps undertaken by various revisionist-ruled countries towards capitalist restoration that I had accumulated since the early 1960s with current facts and figures.

I was pressed to raise further the level of my knowledge on the subject because I was frequently invited to speak on it by groups and organizations in solidarity with the Filipino people and by communist and workers parties and groups.

I was interviewed on the subject by various publications, whether the starting point was the Philippines or the countries that underwent capitalist restoration. I was also asked to contribute articles on the subject by Philippine and foreign publications.

Most important of all, I participated in conferences and seminars organized by communist parties. I presented papers to these gatherings. Of course, anything I wrote on the subject was of interest to the CPP, which eventually issued the comprehensive document, "Stand for Socialism against Modern Revisionism."

2. In being Chairman of the International Conference of Marxist-Leninist Parties and Organizations (ICMLPO), what were your major initiatives?

JMS: When I became Chairman of the International Conference of Marxist-Leninist Parties and Organizations, from 1992 to 1994, my main interest was in promoting Marxism-Leninism and Mao Zedong Thought and bringing up the principles and lessons learned from the theory and practice of continuing revolution under proletarian dictatorship through cultural revolution. My main purpose was to make a stand for socialism against modern revisionism and capitalist restoration.

The ICMLPO had only nine participating parties and groups before I became the chairman in 1992. I took a number of major initiatives to increase the number of participating parties to more than twenty and to hold the International Seminar on Mao Zedong Thought to celebrate the 100th birth anniversary in order to honor the great Mao.

I also proposed in 1994 the formation of an international league of mass organizations in order to parallel and complement the ICMLPO. But then, in 1994, I had no more time to push for the realization of my own proposal. Later in 1998 I would be able to form the International Initiative Committee to found the International League of Peoples' Struggle (ILPS) eventually in 2001.

3. Can you describe the significance of the celebration of the 100th birth anniversary of Mao Zedong under the auspices of the ICMLPO in Germany in 1993?

JMS: We, in the ICMLPO, deliberately held the International Seminar on Mao Zedong Thought to showcase the worldwide significance not just of Mao's teachings that led to the victory of the people's democratic revolution and socialism. We also aimed to present his teachings concerning the theory and practice of continuing revolution under proletarian dictatorship through the Great Proletarian Cultural Revolution(GPCR). Through the seminar, we highlighted the principles, methods and lessons in combating modern revisionism, preventing the restoration of capitalism and consolidating socialism.

Excellent papers on the various aspects of Marxism-Leninism-Mao Zedong Thought were presented by the representatives of communist parties and groups from several countries in various continents. All these were collected in book form under the title *Mao Zedong Thought Lives*, with Stefan Engels of the Marxist-Leninist Party of Germany (MLPD) and myself as general co-editors.

The seminar and book constituted a major effort to uphold, defend and advance the theory and practice of Marxism-Leninism-Maoism and the cause of socialism against the ideological triumphalism and offensives of US imperialism and its camp followers upon the collapse of the Soviet Union and the full restoration of capitalism in former socialist countries.

4. The Chinese Communist Party took the lead in criticizing Soviet modern revisionism from the early 1960s onwards and Mao put forward the theory and practice of continuing revolution under the dictatorship of the proletariat through the Great Proletarian Cultural Revolution. Obviously China itself has brought down the flag of socialism. How could that ever happen?

JMS: On its own account, the theory of continuing revolution under proletarian dictatorship and the practice of the Great Proletarian Cultural Revolution (GPCR) won great victories before suffering defeat from the Dengist counterrevolution. If not for the GPCR, the entire Chinese socialist revolution would have been defeated earlier by the modern revisionists and capitalist-roaders like Liu Shaoqi and Deng Xiaoping. The positive and negative lessons that can be learned from the GPCR would be impossible without the GPCR occurring and prevailing for ten years.

The GPCR showed how to combat modern revisionism, prevent the restoration of capitalism and consolidate socialism at least for a decade. It was the greatest democratic movement of mass education and mass mobilization in history. There were socialist reforms undertaken in every sphere. These should be studied for further improvement in building and consolidating socialism in the future. Mao thought that it was not enough to conduct one cultural revolution to cope with the danger of capitalist restoration but a series of cultural revolutions until communism is reached.

But there were mistakes that would lead to the defeat. These need to be learned. Under the leadership of Mao the Chinese Communist Party deliberately sought to avoid harsh administrative measures. But there were Rightists who sabotaged the mass movement as well as "Left" elements who raised the Red flag only to run it down. The serious offenders were rehabilitated and even restored to positions of power. Deng Xiaoping was rehabilitated and restored to power after showing remorse and promising not to take revenge on comrades.

It would take too long for me to cite all the victories and setbacks, the positive and negative lessons, to learn from the GPCR. But I wish to stress the point that there will be recurrent and new conditions for the cause of socialism to resurge and win victory as a result of the now intensified contradictions among the imperialist powers, and the historical lessons of the GPCR will serve well as a source of lessons in future rounds of socialist revolution and construction.

Without the GPCR, we would not be able to even argue that we have in our hands the initial theory and practice on how to defeat revisionism against the proposition that socialism is hopeless because there is no solution to the disease that is modern revisionism resulting in the restoration of capitalism.

Even when a certain proletarian line is correct and achieves a number of victories verifying its correctness, it can still be defeated by the bourgeoisie at a certain period. Take for example the Paris Commune of 1871. It prevailed for some two months, with the proletariat taking power by force of arms and establishing the prototype of the proletarian revolution. But it was defeated because it committed certain errors, like failing to promptly attack Versailles, calling for elections in which the bourgeoisie could participate, and so on.

Eventually, the lessons of the Paris Commune of 1871 would be lasting and helpful to the victory of the Great October Revolution because Lenin and the Bolsheviks learned them well and became more resolute in the seizure of power by armed force and in wielding and exercising the state power or the class dictatorship of the proletariat over the bourgeoisie.

5. You were also involved in the Brussels Communist Seminar which the Belgian Workers' Party conducted yearly in the aftermath of the Soviet collapse. How different was this seminar from the ICMLPO?

JMS: I was involved in the annual Brussels Communist Seminar (BCS), organized by the Workers' Party of Belgium (PTB) in the 1990s, until recent years in the 21st century. My involvement in the seminar was based on long-running fraternal relations between the CPP and the PTB and friendly relations of anti-imperialist solidarity between the Belgian and Philippine organizations since the 1980s.

There were similarities and differences between the BCS and the ICMLPO. Both sought to promote working-class unity and leadership in the struggle for national liberation, democracy and socialism against imperialism and all reaction. The PTB played a key role as the single BCS organizer, with a consultative group of participating parties. The MLPD also played a key role as the ICMLPO promoter through a Joint Coordinating Group of several parties.

The BCS was more expansive than the ICMLPO and included several scores of parties and groups. It sought to put together communist parties and groups that adhered to Marxism-Leninism and tried to overcome previous labels of convenience, such as pro-Soviet, pro-Chinese, pro-Albanian or otherwise. It did not require adherence to or willingness to learn from Mao Zedong Thought as the ICMLPO did.

In relation to the collapse of the Soviet Union, the BCS served as a platform for the PTB's position of defending Stalin's record of socialist revolution and construction and antifascist struggle and victory and denouncing the revisionism and capitalist restoration under Gorbachov. The BCS was outstanding in bringing to its fold as participants competing Russia-based parties opposed to the capitalist restoration in and collapse of the Soviet Union.

However, the ICMLPO was emphatic on using Mao Zedong Thought and Mao's theory and practice of continuing revolution under proletarian dictatorship through cultural revolution in criticizing and repudiating modern revisionism and capitalist restoration in the Soviet Union and other former socialist countries. The participants of the ICMLPO were predominantly self-acknowledged Mao Zedong Thought parties in the years especially soon after the collapse of the Soviet Union from 1992 onwards.

6. For a while, the Belgian Workers Party was supporting the Korean Workers Party and the DPRK and then stopped supporting them. Why?

JMS: The Belgian Workers Party (WPB) was quite close to the Korean Workers Party (KWP) and the DPRK, especially when the Korean people were suffering gravely from natural calamities in the 1990s. Relative to their strength, the PTB and the BCS gave strong moral, political and material support to the Korean people.

I do not know the details of the bilateral relations of the PTB and the KWP closely enough. Thus, I cannot say anything about how such relations developed positively or negatively. The BCS itself has apparently discontinued since a few years ago because of factors related to the Belgian situation and PTB's priorities in the conduct of its political and electoral struggles.

In recent years, the PTB has been quite successful in the electoral struggle. An increasing number of their candidates to the national and state parliaments and local councils are being elected. The PTB leaders ascribe their success to adjusting their line and methods of work.

7. There certainly has been a strategic setback of the cause of socialism. How can it ever bounce back?

JMS: The socialist cause has suffered a strategic setback since the success of modern revisionism in causing the full restoration of capitalist in the former socialist countries. But the socialist cause will surely bounce back. Since 1991, the crisis of the world capitalist system has become worse and more frequent. It inflicts severe suffering on the proletariat and people and drives them to resist. Consequently, movements for national liberation, democracy and socialism arise and grow against monopoly capitalism and all reaction.

The capitalist restoration in former socialist countries has increased the number of imperialist powers which engage in economic competition and political rivalry. China and Russia have joined the top circle of imperialist powers. Thus, the inter-imperialist contradictions have intensified. The world is afflicted with imperialist crisis, plunder, state terrorism and wars of aggression. The proletariat and people of the world have no choice but to assert their own rights and interests, instead of being simply oppressed and exploited in common by the imperialist powers.

In spite of, or precisely because of, its neoliberal policy of imperialist globalization and its neoconservative policy of ceaseless wars, the US has undermined itself and accelerated its strategic decline. Since the financial meltdown of 2008, it has definitely lost its position of unchallenged sole superpower. It has to reckon with the other imperialist powers in a multipolar world.

In every imperialist country and in every country dominated by imperialism, the big bourgeoisie is running out of effective agents and tools for deceiving and giving false hopes to the proletariat and people. State fascism is outrightly used and fascist movements are being played out to split and mislead the people. But these old tricks of the old capitalist dog are becoming ineffective.

As the oppression and exploitation escalate, the proletariat and people and their leaders and organizations recall the historical experiences that brought about the victories of the movements for national liberation, democracy and socialism; and they adopt and even improve on the successful theory and practice of past revolutionary movements and struggles.

Precisely because of the crisis of the world capitalist system, the theory and practice of Marxism-Leninism-Maoism will guide the resurgent anti-imperialist and socialist cause. The proletarian revolutionary parties, the people's armies, the revolutionary mass organizations, various types of alliances and the organs of political power will arise, grow in strength and advance. The proletariat and the people will rise up to use the most effective methods of struggling against and defeating the enemy.

The very technology the enemy has used to further exploit and oppress the people have accelerated the crisis of overproduction and will be the same weapons for the proletariat and people to seize and use in order to defeat the enemy and liberate themselves. In the process, they will deliberately disable and do away with the means that threaten to destroy humankind by nuclear and environmental catastrophe.

8. It seems that for a long while monopoly capitalism would prevail in the world. How long would it be able to apply neoliberalism to squeeze the most from the proletariat and oppressed peoples?

JMS: Monopoly capitalism will exist for quite a while, in several more decades as we can foresee now, taking into account the still weak status of the revolutionary forces on a global scale. But monopoly capitalism itself, with the aid of higher technology and more effective methods of exploitation and profit-extraction, is driving billions of people to fight back and aim for national and social liberation on an unprecedented global scale.

Neoliberalism as a policy of imperialist globalization is a policy of unbridled greed. It has systematically allowed the monopoly bourgeoisie to squeeze the most from the proletariat and oppressed peoples. By pushing down wage incomes and cutting back on social benefits and social services and providing the monopoly bourgeoisie with further opportunities for profit-taking (tax cuts, trade and investment liberalization, privatization of public assets, deregulation, and denationalization of the underdeveloped economies), the neoliberal policy has led to recurrent and worsening crisis of overproduction which has led in turn to unprecedentedly severe financial crises.

In the entire history of capitalism, the neoliberal policy has caused the largest and fastest transfer of social wealth in the form of debt service and profit remittances from the developing countries to the imperialist countries, the severest aggravation of poverty and biggest social inequality between said types of countries and within each country. It is reported by Oxfam International as of January 2018 that the richest one percent bagged 82 percent of the wealth created in

2017, while the poorest half of humanity got nothing. Credit Suisse data also show that 42 people own the same wealth as the poorest half of humanity.

The imperialist powers themselves are victimized by the neoliberal policy as this leads to global depression and stagnation. No less than the US, the original and main exponent of neoliberalism, is giving it up in favor of protectionism upon its realization that it has undermined itself by conceding consumer manufacturing to China just to ensure its turning into a capitalist country and unwittingly allowing it to raise its level of technology and production in strategic civilian and military goods.

At first from decade to decade and now from year to year, the inter-imperialist contradictions are escalating because of the ever worsening economic and financial crises. These will certainly generate the forces and movements that oppose and strive to overthrow the capitalist system in every country.

9. In case neoliberalism makes people to rebel because of its extreme rule of greed, cannot monopoly capitalism retreat to neo-Keynesianism or social democracy to appease—or rather pacify—the working class and the people again?

JMS: Although they are all fundamentally oppressive and exploitative, the imperialist powers can individually, as a bloc or as a world system, resort to neo-Keynesianism or social democratic policies and measures in order to avoid the consequences of neoliberalism that are adverse even to themselves. They can thus prolong the life of monopoly capitalism. But the imperialist powers individually or collectively can also decide to use fascism to merely suppress the revolutionary forces and the people.

Whatever policy and measures the imperialist powers decide on in an attempt to overcome their socioeconomic and political crisis, the trend of events can run independently of their will because all the objective factors and conditions of crisis are intensifying. They can overestimate or underestimate the strength and potential of the revolutionary forces and adopt the policy that will certainly inflame the revolutionary movement.

Under conditions when the revolutionary forces of oppressed and exploited people are still weak, the imperialist powers seem to be able to prevail forever. But the escalation of oppression and exploitation is unprecedentedly global and intense and the revolutionary forces can grow in strength to such an extent that revolutions can spread fast and widely beyond the control of the imperialist powers. These powers themselves are divided into blocs and can come into conflict with each other and lose control over their respective domains.

10. The threats of inter-imperialist war escalating to nuclear warfare and environmental destruction resulting in an irreversible catastrophe certainly do confront humankind. What can stop either catastrophe?

JMS: The anti-imperialist, democratic and socialist movements of the proletariat and people of the world are the only forces that can prevent nuclear war and environmental catastrophe that threaten the very existence of humankind.

The objective of these movements is not only to serve the working people from national and class exploitation and oppression but also to overthrow the monopoly capitalists who are behind the imperialist threat to wage nuclear warfare and who also engage daily in the wanton plunder of the natural resources and who are bringing about the irreversible environmental catastrophe.

Within an imperialist country that has nuclear weapons and threatens to annihilate humankind, only the proletariat and people can render the nuclear weapons useless. For example, the Soviet social-imperialists could not use their nuclear weapons when the people rose up to overthrow them. Unfortunately, the Russian private monopoly capitalists replaced the bureaucrat monopoly capitalists.

With regard to the need for stopping the ruin of the environment towards irreversible catastrophe, even Bill Gates says that there is no stopping this unless capitalism is replaced by socialism. We can rely on the scientific findings and conclusions that now reveal the phenomenon of global warming and the imminence of environmental catastrophe.

In many parts of the world, the peoples are concerned with the use of fossil fuel and the excessive emission of carbon dioxide that is damaging the ozone layer. Rural-based revolutionary movements and indigenous peoples are now heroically striving to stop open-pit mining, the use of acids to hasten the extraction of mineral ores, rampant deforestation, ill-conceived dam projects, excessive monoculture in agriculture and so many other forms of assault on Mother Nature by monopoly capitalism.

11. Aside from anti-imperialist and class struggle, there are other issues to mind and act upon. What needs to be done about the issues of gender discrimination, racism, ethnicity etc.?

JMS: Issues such as gender discrimination, racism and ethnicity must be taken up on their distinctive accounts. Though these have their own importance, they are somehow related to monopoly capitalism and the need for national and class struggle by the proletariat and the people

While these issues have to be dealt with on their distinctive account, each of them must be understood and handled within the context of social history and circumstances. The problems can be solved only through the revolutionary movement of the proletariat and people which is aimed at national and social liberation from imperialism and all reaction.

Take gender discrimination. This has been generated by the patriarchy and male chauvinism nurtured by the series of class societies, from slavery through feudalism to the current reign of capitalism. Gender discrimination has been perpetuated and fostered by capitalism. It is through the class struggle and the revolutionary movement that women and the LGBTs can achieve liberation and gender equality.

Take racism. In the time of slavery, foreigners and people of other races were treated as barbarians and outside the laws and rules of civility. In wars carried out by all class societies, those who belong to other races were subjected to the worst treatment by the conquerors. It was carried out by all class societies.

In colonizing other countries, as well as establishing colonial settlements, the bourgeoisie of the Western European colonizers perpetuated the most odious forms of racism and genocide. The colonial slave traders kidnapped and killed tens of millions of Africans. The European settlers killed more than 100 million Indians in order to seize their lands and resources. Colonial racism, discrimination and oppression have all been perpetuated by modern imperialism and neocolonialism.

Take ethnicity, local peoples positively assert ethnicity in the face of foreign domination or any kind of imposition from outside. All social and cultural communities are entitled to the inherent and inalienable right to self-determination in the face of an imperialist power or a dominant and oppressive regime within a country. Colonialists and imperialists have manipulated the diversity of ethnic communities in order to divide-and-rule them.

12. You have been chairperson of the ILPS since 2004, after serving as the Chairman of the International Initiative Committee and as General Consultant of ILPS after the Founding Congress. What is the main characteristic of ILPS in contrast to the ICMLPO and the Brussels seminar and what are ILPS' achievements thus far?

JMS: The International League of Peoples' Struggle (ILPS) is an anti-imperialist and democratic league of mass organizations. In organizational form, it is completely different from the Brussels Communist Seminar and the International Conference of Marxist-Leninist Parties and Organizations. These are formations of avowedly Marxist-Leninist parties and groups. Their direct avowal of adhering to Marxist-Leninist ideology makes them different from the ILPS which focuses on anti-imperialist and democratic unity on political, socio-economic and cultural issues at the mass level.

Within the ILPS there are mass organizations and groups that belong to communist and workers parties adhering to Marxism-Leninism. But the ILPS is not the place for focusing on ideological issues. It suffices within ILPS to discuss and decide issues on the common ground of arousing, organizing and mobilizing the people to fight for national liberation, democracy and socialism against imperialism and reaction.

The League fights for the rights and interests of the people in connection with the following concerns:

1. The cause of national liberation, democracy and social liberation;
2. Socioeconomic development and social justice;
3. Human rights in the civil, political, economic, social and cultural fields;
4. The cause of just peace;
5. Independent trade union and workers' and toilers' rights and reduction of working hours at full pay against mass unemployment and decreasing wage levels;
6. Agrarian reform and rights of peasants, farm workers and fisherfolk;
7. The cause of women's rights and liberation;
8. Rights of the youth to education and employment;
9. Children's rights against child labor, sexual abuse and other forms of exploitation;
10. Rights of indigenous peoples, oppressed nations and nationalities against chauvinism and racism;

11. The rights of teachers, researchers and other educational personnel;

12. The right of the people to health care and the rights of health workers;

13. Science and technology for the people and development, and environmental protection;

14. Arts and culture and free flow of information in the service of the people;

15. Justice and indemnification for the victims of illegal arrest and detention;

16. The rights and welfare of displaced homeless persons, refugees and migrant workers;

17. The rights of gays, lesbians, bisexuals and transgendered;

18. The rights of the elderly and the differently-abled; and finally

19. Defense of the environment against imperialist plunder.

The League has achieved so much since its founding in 2001 in making general declarations of peoples' rights and timely statements and resolutions on the burning issues and undertaking international assemblies, seminars, conferences, publications, and global movements and mass actions.

It is made up of more than 300 member-organizations in more than 40 countries in various continents. It has national chapters and global region committees. On varying scales of countries, global regions and the entire world, the ILPS cooperates with allies and partners that are also anti-imperialist, democratic and socialist-oriented.

I served as the Chairman of the International Initiative Committee that founded the ILPS in 2001 and subsequently I became General Consultant until 2004. Since the Second International Assembly in 2004, I have been the Chairperson of the ILPS International Coordinating Committee (ICC) for 15 years. I am stepping down, with the honorific designation as Chairperson Emeritus.

* * *

Chapter IV

The Philippine ruling system after Marcos

1. In general, how do you compare the Marcos regime from the post-Marcos era? Any fundamental change with regard to domestic social conditions and relations with the US?

JMS: There has been no fundamental change from the Marcos to the post-Marcos regimes. Of course, the last 14 years of the Marcos regime was blatant fascist dictatorship. But I describe the post-Marcos regimes as pseudo-democratic because they have perpetuated the same anti-national and anti-democratic ruling system and they have undertaken strategic operational plans to attack and destroy the revolutionary movement of workers and peasants. Their sense of democracy is limited to mutual tolerance among parties of the same exploiting and oppressive classes of big compradors, landlords and bureaucrat capitalists.

The ruling system remains semicolonial and semifeudal operated by the corrupt political agents of the exploiting classes and subservient to US imperialism. There has been no change of social conditions, with the exploiting classes comprising less than two percent of the population but sitting on top of a thin layer of the middle social strata and the overwhelming mass of workers and peasants who comprise more than 90 percent of the population.

There has been no fundamental change in relations with the US. All the treaties, agreements and arrangements that make the Philippines subservient to the US economically, politically, culturally and militarily remain. Against the wishes of the Cory Aquino regime, the Philippine Senate did not extend the US-RP Military Bases Treaty in 1991. But subsequently a series of agreements like the Mutual Support and Logistics Agreement, the Visiting Forces Agreement and the Enhanced Defense Cooperation Agreement have been forged in order to perpetuate US military forces in the Philippines.

Comes Duterte as the most recent president of the reactionary government. Though at first he declared himself "Left" and "socialist," he is actually a rabid dog of US imperialism and the chief representative of the domestic exploiting classes. He became president with the financial support from the Chinese big compradors and the most notorious plunderers and oligarchs of Luzon like the Marcoses, Arroyos, Estradas, Enriles and Revillas. He continued Oplan Bayanihan in 2016 until he launched his own Oplan Kapayapaan in January 2017 in order to pursue an all-out war policy against the revolutionary movement and the people.

At first he pretended to pursue an independent foreign policy. But he has retained all the treaties, agreements and arrangements that make the Philippines subservient to the US. At the same time, he has shown willingness to accept high interest loans and overpriced infrastructure projects from China and make China the dominant partner in the exploitation and development of oil and gas resources in the West Philippine Sea. He has allowed China to build and militarize seven artificial islands in the West Philippine Sea. He is collaborating with two imperialist powers in violating the sovereign rights of the Filipino people and robbing the people of their national patrimony.

2. How do you sum up the Cory Aquino administration? What were the good points and bad ones? Which were dominant?

JMS: Cory Aquino undertook some positive actions at the beginning of her term. She fulfilled her promise to release all political prisoners. She made it a point to repeal some of the most draconian presidential decrees of Marcos and undo their consequences. She sought and made possible a ceasefire agreement with the NDFP in order to prepare the agenda for peace negotiations. She created the Constitutional Commission to draft the 1987 Constitution, which carried some good provisions like those limiting the martial law powers of the president, further guaranteeing human rights and prohibiting foreign military forces and weapons of mass destruction on Philippine territory.

But soon enough she bared the reactionary character of her regime and increasingly adopted policies and engaged in actions inimical to the people. She condoned the Mendiola massacre of peasants and their urban supporters while they were demonstrating near the presidential palace to demand land reform on January 22, 1987. She did not hold the military and police officers to account for the massacre. Instead, she used the massacre as pretext to terminate the ceasefire agreement and, in her own words, to "unsheathe the sword of war", on February 7, 1987. Punitive actions, like abductions and murder of NDF negotiating personnel were carried out. Thus, the armed conflict went back into full swing.

The Aquino regime proceeded to unleash a "total war" against the revolutionary movement and to align the Philippine economy to the US-instigated neoliberal policy. Though Aquino liberalized trade in many ways, the foreign debt accumulated during the time of Marcos became an obstacle to further foreign borrowing, Thus, she had to resort to local borrowing. She reinforced the semifeudal character of the Philippine economy under a foreign and feudal system of exploitation. Corruption also ran rampant. And this was used by the CIA and the pro-US reactionary military officers to intimidate her by engaging in coup attempts against her regime.

3. Did you ever feel indebted to Cory Aquino for her act of releasing you from prison? Why and how did your relations sour up? Did they ever improve after she cancelled your passport in 1988?

JMS: I was thankful to Cory Aquino for fulfilling her promise to comply with a pre-election agreement with all anti-Marcos forces to release all political prisoners. But I never felt indebted beyond her fulfilment of that particular promise. Had she not done so, she would have discredited herself from the very start of her regime as someone who did not know how to comply with an agreement. She invalidated all the martial law proclamations, orders and decrees that Marcos used to detain and try all oppositionists, especially because she wanted to rehabilitate the memory of her late husband legally and politically.

My relations with Aquino soured upon the deterioration of Aquino's policies and acts against the revolutionary movement, especially after she unsheathed the sword of war. In my public speaking tour abroad, I had to criticize and condemn the increasingly reactionary character of her regime and called her—among others—a sugarcoated blade. It should be kept in mind that Mrs. Aquino allowed the proliferation of various vigilante groups like the Alsa Masa, CAFGU and fanatical armed cults, even praising them as the "embodiment of people power." When the influence of the most reactionary officers over her increased, especially after General Renato de Villa became personally close to her, she had a subversion case filed against me on September 15 and had my passport cancelled the following day.

My relations with Cory Aquino seemed to improve when she was being threatened with several coup attempts in 1989 because she sent our mutual friend, Rep. José V. Yap to visit me in The Netherlands and explore the possibility of peace negotiations between the GRP and the

NDFP. Upon my advice, the NDFP agreed to hold peace negotiations and insisted on a foreign neutral venue because of the bad experience of the NDFP with GRP punitive actions after Aquino terminated the ceasefire agreement in February 1987. But it was the military mutiny headed by Col. Noble, former deputy commander of President Aquino's presidential guards, in Mindanao in December 1989 that discouraged Aquino from pursuing the peace negotiations.

4. How do you sum up the administrations that followed, such as those of Fidel Ramos, Joseph Estrada and eventually Gloria Macapagal-Arroyo? What were their good points and bad ones, respectively? How did they deal with you?

JMS: Having won the presidency in 1992 with a plurality vote of only 23.5 percent, Ramos was eager to soften his image as a military man, to assemble a "rainbow coalition" and to engage the NDFP in peace negotiations. Thus, he sent back Rep. Yap to me to explore peace negotiations with the NDFP. And on September 1, 1992, The Hague Joint Declaration was forged as the framework for peace negotiations. Despite the continuity of the armed conflict, the GRP and the NDFP negotiating panels were able to hammer out 10 major agreements from 1994 to 1997.

The Ramos regime conformed to the US-imposed neoliberal policy and was able to access loans from Japanese and Western creditors to generate a boom in private construction and to cover large consumer imports. It also sold prime government land and government corporations in the oil trade and in steel semi-processing in order to fund a rising government budget. It boasted of a high GDP growth rate. Then came the 1997 Asian financial crisis to burst Ramos' kind of economic bubble.

Estrada appeared to be friendly with the NDFP in the early months of his regime. He signed the Comprehensive Agreement on Respect for Human Rights and International Humanitarian Law (CARHRIHL), which Ramos as GRP principal did not sign. But Estrada terminated the peace negotiations in May 1997 when he resented the NPA's capture of General Victor Obillo and the NDFP criticism of the Visiting Forces Agreement, which Estrada entered into with the US in 1999.

Under Estrada, the Philippine economy was severely weakened by the Asian financial crisis, by the drastic reduction of semimanufactured exports (mainly semiconductors) and by the scarcity of foreign credit.

Estrada became notorious for corruption by using social insurance or pension funds to finance gambling operations and other enterprises from which he collected bribes, and for lording over the nationwide illegal numbers game (*jueteng*). He was impeached by the Lower House of Congress. Then he was soon overtaken by the mass protests, which compelled him to leave the palace and in effect resign from his position.

Gloria Macapagal-Arroyo followed the pattern of appearing to be friendly to the NDFP for a few months and willing to resume the peace negotiations. She was aware that she had become president from being vice president because the mass protests of the national democratic movement had ousted Estrada from his office. She and I concurred to avail of the Royal Norwegian Government (RNG) as the third party facilitator. Thus, the peace negotiations were resumed upon the reaffirmation of all previous agreements. Aside from this, the guidelines for the implementation of CARHRIHL were mutually approved and the Joint Monitoring Committee was formed.

The peace process seemed to be running smoothly until the military pressed Arroyo to suspend the negotiations indefinitely by invoking as pretext the death of a notorious human rights violator, Governor Rodolfo Aguinaldo of Cagayan province, who resisted NPA arrest. Thereafter, Arroyo escalated the military offensives under Oplan Bantay Laya against the NPA and other revolutionary forces; and carried out "legal offensives" to frame up legal social activists for indefinite detention and murder.

The Arroyo regime benefited from the loosening of international credit to counter the stagnation effect of the Asian financial crisis. The boom in private construction thus resumed and China increased orders for semiconductors from the Philippines because it had taken up the slack in manufacturing by the so-called Southeast Asian economic tigers and had thereby emerged as the final platform for assembling electronic products for export to the US and other Western markets. Before the Arroyo regime ended, it had already felt the strong negative impact of the financial meltdown of 2008, which emanated from the US and the European Union. Among this was the fall in the already unjustly and exploitatively low prices of Philippine raw-material exports, such as crude coconut oil and copra meal, which brought down copra prices even further.

5. I understand that, as far as Estrada is concerned, you had frequent jousts with him, especially over the radio waves. Did he take any hostile action against you?

JMS: I had almost daily jousts with Estrada over the radio waves and in the print media after he terminated the peace negotiations in May 1999. I went against his high popularity rating originating mainly from his having been a movie star. But he discredited himself with his blatant acts of corruption and weakened his regime financially by waging all-out war against the MILF and overshooting the budgetary limits set by the IMF.

At that time, as in the present, the Philippine economy and finance were under IMF oversight and management in line with Article IV of the IMF's Articles of Agreement, requiring compliance of the Philippine with policy dictates of yearly missions and "consultations:" by IMF officials representing Wall Street.

I had fun lambasting Estrada for his corruption and for posing as a false and fat and wobbly version of Rambo. I had the whole country with me laughing at his expense when I called him Rambotete, to ridicule him for being a false copycat of the tall and muscular Sylvester Stallone. The humor went well with my serious criticisms of his corruption, his misuse of the reactionary armed forces against the MILF and the NPA and his bungling the budget of the reactionary government.

Obviously, Estrada had no sense of humor. Soon enough, he directed his hatchetmen to design an assassination plot against me and to dispatch a sequence of two hit teams to The Netherlands. The first hit team could not accomplish its mission and ended up discouraged because it could not solve the problem of getting close enough to knife or hack me according to plan. The second hit team saw me crossing the street in front of the office but was foiled upon sight of another comrade trying to catch up with me.

I was able to get earlier most of the information about the hit teams from someone who backed out of the plot from the first hit team before Col. Reynaldo Berroya exposed the plot over the DZBB program of Mike Enriquez in January 2001 and came over to The Netherlands in February 2001, to give the details of the plot to the Utrecht police in the company of my Filipino lawyer, the late Atty. Romeo T. Capulong, and myself.

6. It was during Arroyo's term that several "legal offensives" were taken against you in the Philippines and abroad. What were these and why did they occur?

JMS: For every incident in which the NPA was allegedly involved, the military under the Arroyo regime charged me with common crimes, like murder, robbery and arson, in violation of the jurisprudence that I could be charged only with simple rebellion if there was any evidence that I had something to do with the NPA actions.

But those charges were worthless because I could not be arrested by virtue of my being recognized as a political refugee. They were used only for psywar. My status abroad as a recognized political refugee was different from those who were in the Philippines and were more vulnerable to threats to life, arbitrary arrest, torture, prolonged detention and even death.

The Arroyo regime was more effective in its mischief against me by undertaking its "legal offensive" abroad. In November 2001, when she went to Washington, Arroyo formally made the request to the US to designate the CPP, NPA and myself in particular as "foreign terrorists." When US state secretary Colin Powell visited Manila within the first week of August 2002, he was reminded of the request for the designation of the aforesaid as foreign terrorists. Upon his return to Washington, he complied with the request on August 9, 2002.

The immediate consequence to me in The Netherlands was my being listed as a terrorist subject to sanctions by the Dutch government. My bank account was frozen. I contested the listing and demanded evidence as basis for the listing and sanctions. The evidence so-called was flimsy and worthless.

So, the Dutch government delisted me but proceeded to be the prime movant in the European Council for my name to be included in the EU terrorist list on October 22, 2002. The Dutch government persisted in freezing my account and proceeded to withdraw my social benefits, including living allowance, housing, health insurance and pension.

One more "legal offensive" that the Arroyo regime undertook against me was requesting the Dutch government to charge me with using Dutch territory to conspire with others in the Philippines to murder a number of persons. Thus, I was arrested by the Dutch police on August 28, 2007. And the arrest also served as the pretext for raiding the NDF Information Office, my apartment and the homes of seven other Filipinos in fishing for evidence not only for the charge of murder but also for the EU terrorist listing. But no such evidence was found.

I was put in solitary confinement for a total of 17 days. I was released on September 13, 2007 for insufficiency of evidence. But the Dutch authorities appealed the case to the Appellate Court in The Hague which decided on October 4, 2007 that I should remain free because of insufficient evidence. However, the Court authorized the Dutch prosecution service to continue the investigation of my case.

Ultimately, the European Court of Justice decided on September 30, 2009 to remove my name from the EU terrorist list because of the violation of my rights to be informed of the charge, to legal counsel and judicial review before the imposition of sanctions. The decision became final on December 10, 2009. And shortly thereafter, the Dutch Prosecution Service finally stopped the investigation of the false charges of murder against me.

7. Back in summer 2010, Benigno S. Aquino III, assumed the presidency. He obviously had the same trajectory as Arroyo in dealing with you, at first friendly and then hostile. Why in the case of Aquino?

JMS: Like Arroyo, Aquino II took the stance of being interested in the peace negotiations in order to impress the people and the peace advocates, including the progressive intelligentsia and the religious. He was also taking the chance to show friendliness to the revolutionary movement and to explore possibilities of settlement in favor of his regime and the ruling system, while he consolidated power by appointing his partisans in the bureaucracy and promoting the military officers he favored.

Also like Arroyo, Aquino II turned hostile when he became increasingly subject to daily intelligence briefings and advice from the security cluster of the Cabinet. As in Arroyo's time, he was under advice from the military that he should obtain across the negotiating table what could not be won in the battlefield. The repeated military formula for the president was to block serious negotiations on the social, economic and political reforms needed for a just peace and to entice the NDFP to agree to a protracted ceasefire agreement, like that with the MNLF and the MILF, in order to paralyze the NPA and the revolutionary movement.

Again, like Arroyo, Aquino II had to bend to the wishes of the US-lining military officers to avert any threat from them and gain more time for reaping financial benefits from pork barrel deals with congressmen and senators and from the grant of contracts and privileges to private corporations. Ultimately, he was overwhelmed by bureaucratic corruption and the military pressure to pursue Oplan Bayanihan, the strategic plan to destroy the revolutionary movement, because the NDFP could not be made to accept protracted ceasefire agreement prior to comprehensive agreements on social, economic and political reforms.

The Aquino II regime sought to destroy the revolutionary movement with Oplan Bayanihan and perpetrated gross and systematic human rights violations, especially in the countryside. The Aquino aversion to land reform was highlighted by his escalation of military campaigns of suppression in the countryside and, of course, by his frenzied efforts to reverse the application of land reform on Hacienda Luisita (owned by the Aquinos and Cojuangcos) by brute force, muddling the list of land reform beneficiaries and offers of leaseback to the farm workers.

The application of the neoliberal economic policy deepened under the regime of Benigno Aquino III. He continued Arroyo's policy of raising the value-added tax to jack up state revenues at the expense of the consuming public and benefited from the inflow of hot money or portfolio investments, which together with new foreign loans, served to maintain import-dependent consumption and cover deficits in foreign trade. The hot money surged in, driven as it was by low interest rates in the US and other imperialist countries; and by the hunger for higher returns in the financial market in the Philippines.

The annual GDP growth rate increased but the GDP consisted of rising government expenditures, import-dependent consumption and investments in private construction and semi-manufacturing – not in genuine industrialization. As a result, the underdeveloped character of the Philippine economy deepened and was aggravated even further. This absence of national industrialization was exposed by the outflow of the hot money starting 2014 in response to rising US interest rates.

The Philippine economy remained agrarian yet it could not produce enough food staples for itself because of the liberalized importation of these and the chronic dependency on imported rice and wheat for bread undermined domestic food production. At the same time, foreign mining, wood, agrochemical and plantation companies ravaged the

Philippine economy and the environment. The big compradors and their foreign principals had their heyday and happy times in private construction and semi-manufacturing at the expense of the people and the economy.

One good point worth mentioning about the Aquino II regime is that, after great pressure from the people and mass organizations, it filed a case against China for claiming the West Philippine Sea and violating the sovereign rights of the Philippines to its exclusive economic zone and extended continental shelf in accordance with the UN Convention on the Law of the Sea.

Another good point of the regime was the arrest and detention of plunderers like former president Arroyo and others upon the prodding of the mass movement. Still another good point was the continued effort to recover the ill-gotten wealth of the Marcoses and to indemnify the Marcos victims of human rights violations.

But on the whole, the bad points of the Aquino regime outweighed its good points. Aquino continued and exacerbated the neoliberal economic policy and unleashed the US-designed Oplan Bayanihan, a strategic plan to destroy the revolutionary movement. These basic policies of the regime inflicted more exploitation and oppression on the toiling masses of workers and peasants.

8. At first you had high hopes for the long-time Mayor of Davao City, Rodrigo Duterte. Why was this so in the first place, given his dark track record as regards human rights in that city? What happened subsequently that eventually led to a deep estrangement between both of you?

JMS: We in the NDFP had high hopes that Duterte would fulfill his electoral promises, especially the amnesty and release of all political prisoners, and prove his self-description as Left and socialist through his policies and actions as president and through the GRP-NDFP peace negotiations as the GRP principal. For the first time in Philippine history, here was a presidential candidate proclaiming himself as Left and socialist. We had to allow him to unfold before we could call him a political swindler.

Of course, there was his political background in Davao City. There were mixed reviews about him. He was supposed to have cooperated with the revolutionary movement in his home city and region.

The comrades in Southern Mindanao region confirmed his having cooperated with them for a long period but they also described him as a self-interested bureaucrat capitalist who had enriched himself by pocketing public funds and smuggling drugs and other taxable goods at the Davao City port and that he was probably engaged in extrajudicial killings and other human rights violations. But they also said that although he caused the killing of hundreds of suspected drug users and peddlers, the Human Rights Commission had not gathered enough evidence to bring a case to court.

The Left electoral alliance, Makabayan Bloc, actually supported the presidential candidate Grace Poe, not Duterte. But she lost the election despite being No. 1 candidate up to February 2016. But she was timid in denouncing the outgoing Aquino regime and its presidential candidate Mar Roxas. She was surpassed by Duterte in using vitriolic language against the Aquino II regime and its presidential candidate and in harping demagogically that he could solve the illegal drug problem, crime and corruption within a short time by killing the culprits.

Behind the scene, Duterte received plenty of campaign money from the Chinese lobby, his compadre Peter Lim and other big drug lords and the worst Luzon-based plunderers—the Marcoses, Arroyos, Estradas, Enriles, Revillas and others who provided him with votes from their respective electoral bailiwicks and with money from their own secret accounts and financiers. It is not true that the CPP, NPA and the revolutionary movement made Duterte president. It was the alliance of plunderers that gave their bailiwick votes to augment the Visayas vote for Duterte.

What first disgusted the NDFP and myself, all revolutionary forces and all legal patriotic and progressive forces, the religious, human rights activists, and peace advocates was his reneging on his promise to amnesty and release all political prisoners after assuming the presidency. Soon after he became president, he announced that he would not fulfill his promise because he would lose all his bargaining chips if he did so.

Thus, even as the peace negotiations seemed to advance from one round of formal talks to another and he even appointed some progressives on their individual merits to his cabinet, the NDFP could no longer trust Duterte's word. This would be confirmed by a series of his arrogant and bellicose actions, like putting the demand for a protracted ceasefire ahead of the substantive agenda of social, economic and political reforms, unleashing his all-out war against the revolutionary forces and repeatedly terminating the peace negotiations.

9. Does Mr. Duterte hold any personal animosity to you? How do you react to his rants against you?

JMS: It is possible that he bears a personal animosity towards me, because of his anticommunist bias, his reactionary interests as an oligarch and his violations of human rights.

I laugh at Duterte's frequent rants against me because they are shallow and vulgar. He cannot really raise any serious issue against me. His rants have become the occasion for me to issue serious statements in the interest of the Filipino people against his tyrannical, treasonous, murderous, corrupt and swindling policies and actions against the people.

10. You have consistently been a sharp critic of all the presidents from Marcos to Duterte. Did you ever entertain presidential ambitions yourself? Why or why not?

JMS: I have criticized all presidents from Marcos to Duterte because I take a principled stand for the people's democratic revolution and against the semicolonial and semifeudal ruling system. The presidents cited have been no more than traitorous and greedy political agents of US imperialism and the local exploiting classes of big compradors, landlords and bureaucrat capitalists. They are opposed to the national and democratic rights and interests of the people.

Once upon a time, at the age of ten from the time I started to top my classes in grade school, I wished to become president because my father encouraged me to become a lawyer and eventually president. There was also the influence cast by relatives who had occupied high positions at the municipal, provincial and national levels of the government from Spanish colonial times to the present.

But at the age of 18 to 19, I advanced from being a progressive liberal in the university to a Marxist-Leninist committed to the cause of continuing the unfinished Philippine revolution along the line of the people's democratic revolution with a socialist perspective. I repudiated the ruling system and proceeded to do whatever I could in order to advance the revolutionary cause among students and then among the workers and peasants in quick succession in the early 1960s.

When Duterte boasted that he must be more intelligent than me because he is president, whereas I am not, I had a good laugh at my former mediocre student in the Lyceum of the Philippines. In riposte, I said that Claro Mayo Recto was superior in intellect to anyone who had become president but he could not become president for the simple reason the he was anti-imperialist and that US imperialism and other big election campaign financiers would not allow him to become president.

I said that since the age of 19, I have never aspired to become president because I have committed myself to the resumption of the Philippine revolution and to the overthrow of the exploitative and oppressive ruling system. Since the age of 22, I have been considered a national newsmaker because of my activism and writings.

In the latter half of the 1960s when I was still less than 30 years old and not yet of age to run for the Senate I was much amused when both the Liberal Party and the Nacionalista Party conventions listed me as one of the nominees for Senator because of my high rate of name recognition as leader of Kabataang Makabayan.

I also had a good laugh when under military detention I was listed in 1985 by the Kongreso ng Mamamayang Pilipino (KOMPIL) as one of the 15 top Filipinos who could replace Marcos as president in response to his boast that he was irreplaceable. The Group of 15 was highly honorable as it included senior eminences like Lorenzo Tañada, José W. Diokno and even Jaime Cardinal Sin. At any rate, I was inspired and encouraged by the high regard extended to me by the congress.

11. Short of seizing political power in Manila, what are the possibilities of a peace agreement or an anti-imperialist and progressive leader emerging from the system?

JMS: Aside from the possibility of the revolutionary movement overthrowing the ruling system and seizing power in Manila, a peace agreement becomes realizable if and when the legal forces of the national democratic movement or a coalition of patriotic and progressive forces take leadership over the reactionary government.

But this possibility is far-fetched at the moment. For the GRP and the NDFP to reach a peace agreement, the leadership of the GRP has to be truly independent of US imperialism and willing to cooperate in the realization of basic social, economic and political reforms.

Otherwise there is no substitute for the revolutionary forces and people striving or and winning the new democratic revolution. Their growth in strength and advances can be the very condition for the reactionary government to sue for peace. Otherwise, they can proceed to win total victory in the revolution.

* * *

Chapter V

Further development of the Philippine revolution

1. Why did Marcos fail to destroy the armed revolutionary movement, contrary to his scheme that martial law and authoritarian law would finish the movement? In 1981 he launched Oplan Katatagan (Stability). What happened to it?

JMS: Marcos failed to destroy the armed revolutionary movement because he was hated by the people for his brutality and corruption. His scheme of martial law and authoritarian rule could not finish the movement but instead drove the people to resist his regime and the most revolutionary of them who were fit for fighting joined the New People's Army.

Soon after the NPA was founded on March 29, 1969, Marcos was jolted by the successful tactical offensives carried out by the NPA in the second district of Tarlac province. He launched the very first operational plan to try to destroy the NPA. It was code named Oplan Prophylaxis, whose objective was to nip the armed revolution in the bud.

The office of the CPP Central Committee in Sta. Rita, Capas, Tarlac was targeted. My comrades and I were in the barrio. But because of the people's support, we were able to get out of the barrio and frustrate the military operation. The NPA continued to launch tactical offensives and increased its automatic rifles from only nine to more than 200 in one year and a half.

By the time that Marcos launched Oplan Katatagan (Stability) in 1981, the CPP and the NPA had expanded nationwide and taken deep roots in the regions of Ilocos-Montañosa-Pangasinan, Cagayan Valley, Central Luzon, Southern Tagalog, Bicol, Western Visayas, Central Visayas, Eastern Visayas, Eastern Mindanao, Northern Mindanao, Southern Mindanao and Western Mindanao.

Oplan Katatagan increasingly failed to defeat the NPA but succeeded in pushing the people to join and support the armed revolution. This coincided with the worsening socioeconomic and political crisis of the ruling system and the Marcos fascist regime. The land frontier for spontaneous resettlement by the surplus rural population had been exhausted since 1969. There were many landless peasants and farm workers eager to join the people's war.

Marcos had abused foreign borrowing to finance corruption-laden infrastructure projects. The people were rising up both against state terrorism and more intense exploitation. The mass protest actions were increasing and expanding until 1986 when Marcos was overthrown by the uprisings of the people in the millions.

2. How did the armed movement counter and prevail over the enemy scheme for its destruction?

JMS: The CPP adopted the strategic line of protracted people's war for the NPA to pursue. This line avails of the countryside as the wide area where the NPA can grow from small and weak to big and strong over a protracted period of time. Availing of the countryside also means availing of the peasant masses who comprise the majority of the people.

The NPA cannot be built in stages by fighting in the cities. To start the people's war or carry it out prematurely in the cities would certainly result in the destruction of the people's army in a short while, with no hope at all of prevailing over the far superior police and armed forces of the enemy.

Where the NPA could start only with a small and weak force, it had to build a mass base among the peasants and carry out basic guerrilla tactics. It had to engage in mass work in order to encourage the formation of various types of mass organizations, the local organs of political power and the local branch of the CPP and the people's militia.

From the very start of the people's war, the CPP and NPA gave politico-military training for cadres and Red fighters intended to create new CPP regional committees, regional operational commands and new guerrilla fronts. The objective was to frustrate the enemy by nationwide Party and people's army expansion so that the enemy could not concentrate on one or a few guerrilla fronts to destroy them without giving up space and initiative to more guerrilla fronts elsewhere.

Even when the NPA was still building guerrilla zones, it was capable of preserving itself and seizing weapons from the enemy by using basic guerrilla tactics. After the guerrilla fronts, consisting of guerrilla bases and zones arose by the tens and then by the scores in 17 regions in the country, the enemy could no longer concentrate on any number of guerrilla fronts without giving up space and initiative to so many other guerrilla fronts.

In the latter half of the 1970s during the Marcos fascist dictatorship, the NPA had already established guerrilla fronts in so many areas that the military and police forces were no longer capable of effectively attacking all of them at the same time or even by concentrating on one or several guerrilla fronts at the same time without yielding the space and initiative to the NPA in many other areas. The NPA was able to operate at will in 80 percent of the Philippines while the enemy forces had hardly the capacity to occupy even only 10 percent of all the villages at the same time.

3. What were the accomplishments of the revolutionary movement during the time of the Marcos dictatorship?

JMS: The main achievements of the revolutionary movement included the building of the CPP as the leading party, the NPA, the NDF, the underground mass organizations, the alliances of various types and scales and the local organs of political power which constituted the base of the people's democratic government.

These were the organized forces of the revolutionary movement. They stood at the core of the broad masses of the people. They ensured that the masses were aroused, organized and mobilized to be the most effective in developing the people's resistance to the fascist dictatorship. They undermined and isolated it in a cumulative way until the legal urban-based mass organizations would arise in full force in order to overthrow it in 1986.

The role played by the revolutionary movement was crucial and decisive in bringing about the downfall of Marcos. The Aquino-type of opposition and all anti-Marcos reactionaries were ineffective for a long while and were too dependent on the hope and calculation that the US would junk Marcos after proving himself more of a liability than an asset to the US. It was the growing strength of the armed revolutionary movement that ultimately persuaded the US, the Catholic Church and most of the big compradors and landlords to junk Marcos.

4. To what extent did errors and shortcomings limit or reduce the achievements of the movement? Why was what you call the Second Great Rectification Movement (SGRM) in the early 1990s necessary?

JMS: There were major errors that had consequences detrimental to the revolutionary movement and to some extent limited the achievements of the movement. They were Right and "Left" opportunist errors, which sprang from the subjectivist notion that the Marcos dictatorship had already industrialized the Philippines and that the strategic line of protracted people's war was already invalid.

The Right opportunists in 1981 wanted to build a bourgeois-liberal New Katipunan, a recycling of the old democratic revolution, to take out the working class leadership supposedly to satisfy the anti-Marcos reactionary allies and thereby attract more people and to make the legal struggle the principal form of struggle. Of course, the Right opportunist current was a short-lived virus because they were trying to reverse the line of people's war predominantly set and carried out by the Maoist cadres and Red fighters nationwide.

The "Left" opportunists caused far more damage to the revolutionary movement than the Right opportunists because they posed as the more effective armed revolutionaries by pushing the line of urban insurrectionism, giving highest priority to a combination of people's strikes and armed city partisan operations as the lead factor and reducing the NPA to being a purely military force, good only for checkpoints and containing actions.

The worst of "Left" opportunism was the rapid formation of absolutely concentrated NPA companies from three to 16 in the years of 1981-85 in Mindanao by dissolving the relatively dispersed smaller formations doing mass work. Up to the 5th company in 1984 the wrong line seemed to be correct but thereafter, the further increase of companies made the NPA less effective and more subject to isolation and enemy offensives.

Instead of analyzing, criticizing and correcting their wrong line, the "Left" opportunists covered it up, blaming supposed "deep penetration agents" (DPAs) as responsible for the setbacks and launched "Kampanyang Ahos" to ferret them out. They generated an anti-DPA hysteria and punitive actions without due process against CPP cadres, NPA Red fighters, mass activists and allies who were being accused as being DPAs without sufficient evidence.

They arrested as many as 1,500 suspects and executed hundreds of them without due process and under such barbaric conditions that suspects were subjected to torture, on the basis of forced admissions and hearsay testimonies. Crimes were committed in complete disregard of the tradition and principle that even captive enemy combatants must be treated kindly and cannot be punished arbitrarily.

"Kampanyang Ahos" and similar campaigns in four regions at various times resulted in serious damage to the revolutionary movement. There were decreases in armed strength and mass base in adversely affected areas, which became conspicuous in 1987 and 1988. The overwhelming majority of good CPP members and NPA commanders and fighters and revolutionary activists started to demand action against the "Left" opportunist line. In the years of 1988 onwards, when the central leadership called for a rectification movement, the "Left" and Right opportunists tended to support each other and threatened to do wrecking operations within the Party.

By late 1991, the central leadership of the CPP was determined to launch the Second Great Rectification Movement (SGRM) and launched it in 1992 with the main document, "Reaffirm our Basic Principles and Rectify Errors." The rectification movement had to be waged as a basically educational campaign in Marxism-Leninism-Maoism and in the strategy and tactics in order to reaffirm basic principles, criticize and repudiate the errors and revitalize the entire revolutionary movement.

Had the major subjectivist and opportunist errors been allowed to persist, these would have caused the internal disintegration of the CPP and other revolutionary forces, especially at a time when the revisionist-ruled countries became fully capitalist and the Right opportunists were toying with various ideas, including Gorbachovism, Trotskyism, bourgeois liberalism and even neoliberalism to rationalize their separation from the Party. Thus, the Party leadership had to come up with another major SGRM document, "Stand for Socialism against Modern Revisionism."

5. Since then, how did the movement fare? Any downside?

JMS: The Second Great Rectification Movement (SGRM) ran from 1992 to 1998. The CPP became stronger ideologically, politically and organizationally. The NPA also became a stronger politico-military force. Wherever the major errors of "Left" opportunism resulted in the commission of crimes, CPP cadres and NPA commanders took the lead in apologizing to the surviving victims and the masses as well as to survivors of victims who had been unjustly executed.

The revolutionary movement also extended indemnification to the victims and survivors. Thus, it could recover most of the areas that were vacated as a result of the anti-DPA hysteria. Many of those misled by the principal "Left" opportunists were repentant and reaffirmed their commitment to the revolutionary movement.

The downside of the SGRM was that the Right opportunists who operated foreign-funded NGOs and used the mass base of the revolutionary movement for their projects, usurped and privatized the NGOs for themselves. They also sought and took posts in the reactionary government. The "Left" opportunists who committed the worst crimes, either took away or wrecked that part of the movement of which they had taken hold. They were expelled from the Party but could not be subjected to prosecution and trial by the people's court because they escaped and even joined the reactionary government, including its intelligence services.

The main reasons why certain opportunists could delay the rectification movement from 1988 to 1992 were the same reasons why they could escape responsibility and avoid due process within the Party as well as due process before the people's court (in cases of crimes committed). They were in high central and regional positions and controlled whole organs or offices and operated them like "independent kingdoms." They blocked investigations, generated their own propaganda and ran away with personnel and resources when they were already isolated. True to the Maoist tradition of rectification, the CPP deliberately avoided use of pre-emptive administrative and punitive measures but laid stress on internal debate, persuasion and education.

By 1994, most of those misled by the "Left" and Right opportunists had returned to the Party. By 1996, the CPP and NPA forces in Mindanao were outstanding in taking the SGRM seriously from the beginning. They rectified errors and overcame the consequent damages. By 1998, the CPP announced the complete victory and conclusion of the SCRM nationwide. By 1999 the NPA had the signal honor of capturing an AFP brigadier general in Mindanao. By 2000, the urban-based mass movement, especially the workers' and youth organizations were stronger than ever before and would play the key role in the ouster of Estrada from the presidency in 2001.

6. The administration of Corazon Aquino started with Oplan Mamamayan (People) in 1986 and proceeded with Oplan Lambat

Bitag (Net-Trap) in 1988 as the strategic plan to destroy the NPA. Your former recruit to the CPP and NPA, Victor Corpus, was part of designing Lambat Bitag I. Why and how did these strategic plans fail?

JMS: Oplan Lambat Bitag, the strategic plan of the Aquino I regime to destroy the revolutionary movement utterly failed to realize its objective. It was not even able to take full advantage of the damages wrought by the "Left" opportunist line in several regions from 1985 onward. The CPP's strong Maoist foundation and the prevalence of the good CPP cadres, NPA commanders and fighters and mass activists prevailed nationwide and even caused overall increase in the number of NPA automatic rifles by the hundreds beyond the 6,000 level in 1986 and 1987.

Lambat Bitag involved the identification of the guerrilla fronts and systematic occupation of certain villages for extended periods in order to achieve the "gradual constriction" of the area available for NPA's wide maneuver. Gradual constriction was supposed to result in the NPA's loss of mass base and in compelling NPA forces into a position of passivity and vulnerability to attack by superior enemy forces.

The Lambat Bitag objective to destroy the NPA could not be achieved because the NPA had a far greater number of guerrilla fronts and far wider space for maneuver nationwide than the enemy forces could identify. And neither had the enemy enough forces to concentrate on even only 10 percent of the NPA's mass base and area of maneuver. The enemy forces could not even take advantage of the damages wrought by the "Left" opportunists because most of the guerrilla fronts were in healthy and vigorous condition.

Despite his becoming a CPP member and NPA military trainor for a while, Victor Corpus maintained an idealist and bourgeois mode of thinking and action. He never learned dialectical materialism. Perhaps, he understood that the NPA could use basic guerrilla tactics in every guerrilla front (retreat when a superior enemy force advances, harass when the enemy camps and advance when the enemy retreats). But he never understood that at the level of strategy and campaigns, the NPA had available higher tactics, such as shifting, dispersal and concentration according to need, luring the enemy in deep or using feints to confuse it and also using the unlimited space for maneuver to attack at so many enemy weak points on a nationwide scale.

By the time Lambat Bitag was launched, the NPA had grown to such an extent that it was impossible for the enemy to identify and clamp down on all the NPA units and mass base. In this regard, because of the people's support and participation in the areas, the enemy forces are blind to the actual precise location of nearly all guerrilla units all the time. No amount of the enemy's triad operations (psywar, intelligence and combat) could cure its malignant character as the instrument of the exploiting and oppressive classes.

7. Mr. Ramos tried a mix of war and peace approaches to destroy the movement. Nevertheless, Lambat Bitag was continued. What happened then?

JMS: Ramos was conscious of having to adopt political tactics to widen his support because he had gotten only 23.5 percent of the vote to win the presidency. Upon the advice of House speaker De Venecia and Rep. José V. Yap, he adopted the line of "rainbow coalition" within and outside the government, up to approaching the CPP and NDFP for peace negotiations.

At the same time, he had the illusion that he could make the revolutionary movement capitulate because he was hearing that the CPP was already "in shambles" because of the anti-CPP propaganda of the opportunists who had turned renegades, the worst of whom became sources of enemy intelligence. He had no idea that the CPP was effectively engaged in rectification and prevailing over the opportunist errors and the damage these had caused.

He agreed to the meeting of GRP and NDFP representatives in 1992 and The Hague Joint Declaration of September 1, 1992 was forged as the framework for peace negotiations. On the next day, upon the advice of the military, he created the National Unification Commission headed by Haydee Yorac in order to hold "localized peace talks" and supposedly to induce CPP and NPA personnel to surrender. The military had persuaded Ramos that the CPP and the NPA were in the process of disintegration as reported by renegades.

But the NPA continued to launch tactical offensives nationwide although at a reduced rate in a few regions. Speaker José de Venecia, Rep. José V. Yap and Justice Secretary Silvestre Bello prevailed upon Ramos to dissolve the NUC and resumed preparatory peace talks in 1994. The GRP-NDFP formal peace negotiations were formally opened in Brussels in 1995 after several agreements negotiated in The Netherlands were approved by the Negotiating Panels.

The peace negotiations proceeded even as the civil war continued. But the GRP and NDFP negotiating panels succeeded in arriving at several important agreements, including the Joint Agreement on Safety and Immunity Guarantees (JASIG), the Joint Agreement on the Sequence, Formation and Operationalization of the Reciprocal Working Committees and the Comprehensive Agreement on Respect for Human Rights and International Humanitarian Law (CARHRIHL), the first item in the four-item substantive agenda.

However, Ramos relented on signing the CARHRIHL. He and De Venecia wanted me to return home to attend the signing of the comprehensive agreement. But they did not comply with the NDFP request to release all political prisoners. For that reason I did not return to the Philippines. Time passed until Ramos' presidential term ended.

8. The short-lived administration of Estrada stuck to its own strategic plans – Balangay (Branch) (1999-2001) – to be followed by three phases of Oplan Bantay Laya (Freedom Watch) under Mrs. Arroyo. These were quite bloody, wherever General Jovito Palparan, more commonly referred to as "berdugo" (butcher), was assigned. Furthermore, Mr. Aquino and Mr. Duterte came out with their own plan, dubbed Oplan Bayanihan (Cooperation) and Oplan Kapayapaan (Peace), respectively. How come none of these strategic plans were crowned by ultimate success?

JMS: All the strategic plans intended to destroy the armed revolutionary movement from the time of Estrada to Duterte have failed for definite reasons in general as well as in particular, relative to a reactionary regime.

The general reasons for the failure of all the regimes were as follows: The objective conditions are favorable for people's war because the semicolonial and semifeudal ruling system is in such a grave chronic crisis that it can no longer be ruled in the old way by the traditional politicians of the exploiting classes of big compradors and landlords. The people are desirous of revolutionary change and a revolutionary party of the proletariat is leading them and is growing in strength from the revolutionary struggle.

The CPP is and remains the most important force of the revolution. It is the Party capable of leading the proletariat and the people from the new democratic to the socialist stages of the revolution. It has put forward the general line of people's democratic revolution against the three evil forces of foreign monopoly capitalism, domestic feudalism and bureaucrat capitalism.

It has defined the strategic line of protracted people's war; and it has organized the NPA to integrate revolutionary struggle, agrarian revolution and mass-base building, especially among the peasant masses. It has built the NDF as the most consolidated united front organization, consisting of 18 revolutionary formations representing the toiling masses of workers and peasants and the middle social strata of urban petty bourgeoisie and middle bourgeoisie.

The Estrada regime in particular failed to destroy the revolutionary movement because it was opposed to the national and democratic rights and interests of the people. It was afflicted with economic and financial crisis and scandalously corrupt. It plundered the social insurance funds for public and private employees and lorded over illegal gambling operations. It wasted government funds by launching an all-out war against the Moro Islamic Liberation Front and further limited its armed personnel and resources to fight the NPA. In the time of Estrada the NPA had fully recovered from the damages wrought by the "Left" opportunists, Estrada emerged an easy target for ouster by the urban mass movement and withdrawal of support by his own military.

In the time of Arroyo there was relative recovery from the abrupt drop of economic conditions in the wake of the Asian Financial Crisis of 1997. The finances of the reactionary government were buttressed by foreign and local borrowing and by the imposition of higher value-added tax on consumption goods in order to maintain the high level of import-dependent consumption. Furthermore, the Arroyo regime reeked to high heavens with corruption.

Arroyo unleashed Oplan Bantay Laya against the revolutionary movement, suspected revolutionaries and entire communities in the form of brutal military operations, which resulted in the kidnapping and slaughter of suspects. The repression also took the form of "legal offensives" in which false charges were levelled against suspected political offenders in order to imprison or butcher them. But the Arroyo regime failed to destroy the revolutionary movement and instead only aroused even further revolutionary fervor and efforts by the revolutionary forces nationwide.

The Aquino II regime benefited from foreign borrowing and big inflows of hot money or portfolio investments from the US and other imperialist countries. The resulting surge in dollars supported a high level of import-dependent consumption and government spending characterized by bureaucratic corruption, especially through discretionary funds and the pork barrel. Thus, the GDP was bloated and fattened the foreign monopolies and the big compradors. Aquino unleashed Oplan Bayanihan and carried out very much the same tactics that had been employed by the Arroyo regime.

By this time, the conservatism in the armed revolutionary movement, which in earnest began during the Arroyo regime became more conspicuous in Luzon and the Visayas, with the dwindling level of NPA tactical offensives. The CPP, the NPA and the NDFP were confronted by concentrated enemy attacks and were compelled to find ways to defend themselves and counterattack. The NPA in Eastern Mindanao ultimately suffered the main brunt of enemy attacks but learned how to defeat the enemy forces by using the tactics of counter-encirclement in guerrilla fronts and building more guerrilla fronts in other regions.

By the time the Duterte regime came, the CPP and the NPA in Mindanao had already become so strong that it could and extend support to the weaker regions in Luzon and the Visayas in the form of tested personnel and arms. They did so in the same way that personnel and arms were shifted from Eastern Visayas to Mindanao and other regions from 1979 onwards.

Duterte continued Aquino II's Oplan Bayanihan until the end of 2016, whereupon he unleashed his own Oplan Kapayapaan in January 2017. Since then, Duterte has been vociferously and frenziedly carrying all-out war against the revolutionary movement. He set as target the destruction of the movement before the end of 2018. Then, he reset his deadline to May 2019. At the latest, his own defense secretary Delfin Lorenzana has admitted that the NPA cannot be destroyed before the end of Duterte's term in 2022.

The Duterte regime is notorious for its bloodthirsty calls on the military and police to frame up and kill revolutionary suspects with impunity and to bomb communities and their schools, clinics and other structures. At the same time, he dishes out fake news that NPA fighters are surrendering beyond their supposed number of only 2,000 to 4,000 and that also thousands are being killed. The fake surrenders and fake casualties at the expense of the NPA are meant for psywar and for racketeering purposes of military officers who collect cash rewards for the fake surrenders and fake casualties.

The AFP and PNP are actually losing by simultaneously engaging in summary executions of suspects and staging false encounters. Their deceptions and delusions are already well exposed and are inciting the people to resist the state terrorism and the entire Duterte scheme to impose a fascist dictatorship on the people through de facto martial law nationwide. The end game in this scheme is to push charter change for a bogus kind of federalism that centralizes all powers in the hands of the fascist dictator and lets him handpick his agents among the regional and provincial big compradors, landlords and warlords.

9. The SGRM had the severest criticism for Kampanyang Ahos in Mindanao—truly the darkest chapter in the history of the revolutionary movement. Has there ever been an impartial Truth & Reconciliation Commission to heal the wounds? What made the NPA in Mindanao become far stronger than units in Luzon and the Visayas since the SGRM?

JMS: The SGRM had the most severe criticism of Kampanyang Ahos because as a criminal campaign with the greatest number of victims, unlike similar witchhunts that had far less victims in Negros, Southern Tagalog, the national capital region, Cagayan Valley and so on. The SGRM focused on the ideological, political and organizational errors committed by the "Left" opportunists.

The crimes committed under Kampanyang Ahos and other similar anti-DPA witchhunts were subject to prosecution and trial before the people's court. Only a few of the worst criminal offenders could be prosecuted and tried before the people's court because most of them left the CPP and the NPA and quite a number joined the reactionary government, including its intelligence agencies.

The role of the truth and reconciliation commission was carried out practically within the context of the SGRM. It is possible to have such a commission openly only in a final peace agreement as in South Africa or after the total victory of the revolution. Now under CARHRIHL, there is a Joint Monitoring Committee to which either the GRP or the NDFP submits to the other side complaints about the violations of human rights and international humanitarian law but actions on such complaints of one party against the personnel or units of the other party are still under the exclusive jurisdiction of the party of the accused.

The NPA forces in Mindanao have become stronger than those in either Luzon or the Visayas because it took the SGRM seriously and learned much from the errors of the insurrectionist line and premature regularization through the absolute concentration of unsustainable companies. They learned to make a very productive balance of 70 percent relatively dispersed units for mass work and 30 percent relatively concentrated formations for tactical offensives. The balance between mass work and tactical offensives is correct. Such a balance is necessary for extensive and intensive guerrilla warfare on the basis of ever expanding and deepening mass base.

10. What are the solutions being undertaken to solve the problem of "conservatism" that has afflicted the NPA in Luzon and the Visayas?

JMS: The problem of conservatism is practically the extreme opposite of the other extreme that was "Left" opportunism in the 1980s in certain regions at certain periods. It exaggerates mass work by over-dispersal of the NPA units as armed propaganda teams. Thus the capability for tactical offensives against the enemy military and police forces is drastically reduced. It is wrongly presumed that the NPA is doing well in armed struggle as long as it ensures local peace and order among the people and counteracts local bad elements and local tyrants.

But the NPA cannot grow in this way. It even becomes vulnerable to attacks by the enemy forces. The NPA's reason for being is to build units capable of taking the initiative to launch tactical offensives, and seizing weapons from the enemy forces through ambushes and raids, as soon as the mass base is wide and deep enough for the NPA units to maneuver. When squads and half-squads of the armed propaganda teams are easily squashed by enemy units, even the mass base that they have created eventually disappears.

Now that the problem of conservatism has been identified and understood, the NPA forces in Luzon and the Visayas are now expected to emulate those in Mindanao and launch more tactical offensives in order to seize the arms for creating more guerrilla fronts in clusters of three to five and building full companies as the center of gravity in the guerrilla bases and full platoons in every guerrilla zone of a whole guerrilla front.

11. DND Secretary Lorenzana recently claimed that some NPA commanders and fighters have been redeployed to Luzon and Visayas. How true is this report?

JMS: Well, Lorenzana claims publicly that his troops have arrested a few Visayan-speaking NPA Red fighters in Abra and that a whole NPA platoon from Mindanao is now operating in Aurora province. And he complains that the NPA has taken advantage of the peace negotiations to redeploy NPA fighters from Mindanao to other Philippine islands.

The redeployment from regions where the NPA forces are stronger to regions where these are weaker is very well in accordance with the fine communist tradition of one part of the revolutionary movement helping another part. That is a logical and realistic way for solving the problem of uneven development and for raising the strength of the entire revolutionary movement.

12. What is now the overall status of the revolutionary forces and the current trend in the armed conflict?

JMS: Despite its all-out war, the Duterte regime has failed to destroy the NPA. The NPA is obviously becoming stronger in response to the tyrannical, treasonous, murderous, corrupt and swindling Duterte regime. There has been a marked rise of NPA tactical offensives nationwide since the last quarter of 2018. This is expected to continue as the crisis of the ruling system and the crimes of the Duterte regime worsen.

More and more cadres and mass activists from the ranks of workers, educated youth and urban poor are joining the NPA because of the threat of Red tagging, arrest, torture, murder and other acts of state terrorism and because of the urgent need of the NPA expansion and consolidation of strength and the intensification of the people's war against the Duterte regime.

I have learned from CPP publications that the Second Congress was followed up by a Central Committee plenum to make an all-rounded five-year plan to further develop the CPP, the NPA, the mass organizations and organs of political power in a determined effort to realize the advanced stage of the strategic defensive in order to reach the strategic stalemate.

* * *

Chapter VI

Prolonged exile and legal struggles abroad

1. You have been in exile for more than 32 years since you left the Philippines on October 22, 1986. Do you feel homesick? Any plan or hope of returning home?

JMS: Of course, I have short spells of homesickness sometimes because most of my Filipino comrades, relatives and friends are in the Philippines. I am not homesick too often because as a proletarian internationalist, I am at home in the world, wherever I am abroad. I am in touch with the people in the Philippines because of the efficient means of communications in the digital age. Moreover, I am in a community with the Filipino migrant workers and professionals in The Netherlands. Filipino students abroad and travellers from the Philippines visit me ceaselessly.

In a patriotic and emotional way, I compare myself to Filipino migrant workers who are compelled to stay abroad to earn a living for their family in the Philippines. In my case, I am compelled to stay abroad as a political refugee because of the cancellation of my Philippine passport and the threats to my life and liberty.

The same ruling system and the same military organization that tortured and imprisoned me for nine years are demanding and eagerly waiting for my return at the airport so that I could be at their mercy. At this moment, a tyrant who apes Marcos is wishing that I put myself under his control so that he can slap or kill me because I would never agree to the capitulation of the revolutionary movement.

However, I continue to consider the possibility that the peace negotiations between the GRP and the NDFP would progress to such an extent that substantial agreements are reached and that legal and security guarantees are available and that a sane president of the reactionary government has no more interest to do me any personal harm or commit a malicious act at the expense of the revolutionary movement and myself.

2. You are accused of being safe and enjoying your life abroad. What are actually your conditions of legal and economic existence in The Netherlands? You have devoted a great deal of your time to legal actions as well as political actions against legal obstacles and political persecution?

JMS: I have not been completely safe in The Netherlands, although I am far safer here than if I were in Manila. In 1994, I was threatened by one of the renegades or a dropout from the revolutionary movement in the Philippines. In 1999 and 2000, military officers associated with Estrada sent an assassination team twice to hit me but I did not give them a chance by taking precautions after I received advance insider information about the plot.

Then during the time of Arroyo as president, she and her security advisers waged a "legal offensive" against me by having me designated as a "terrorist" by the US government and consequently the Dutch government also listed me as a "terrorist" in August 2002. False murder charges were also filed against me by the Arroyo regime through the Dutch government in 2007. And I was arrested and detained in solitary for 17 days.

I won all the legal cases for the removal of my name from the Dutch and the EU terrorist listing in 2009 and for the dismissal of the false murder charges against me on October 4, 2007. Further investigation of the murder charges were also stopped in early 2010. But when I was put on the EU "terrorist" list, the Dutch authorities withdrew all my social benefits, including my living allowance, housing, health insurance and pension in early 2003. Despite the removal of my name from the EU terrorist list, my social benefits have not been restored.

I do not live beyond the level of bare subsistence on the basis of meager support from my family and loans from friends. I live on the third floor of a walk-up apartment. My mode of entertainment is watching the TV, using the computer and singing a capella or with karaoke at home and occasionally joining Filipino community parties and solidarity nights during meetings of the International League of Peoples' Struggle.

I have devoted a lot of my time from 1988 to 2009 waging legal struggles and joining political actions against legal obstacles and political persecution. I am very much gratified that I have gotten the best possible lawyers free of charge and I have been supported by Filipino compatriots, Dutch and other foreign friends who formed a committee devoted to my legal defense and political support.

In all my more than three decades in Europe, I have enjoyed most giving lectures and speeches to academic and nonacademic audiences and participating in the GRP-NDFP peace negotiations in Oslo and other European capitals in my capacity as NDFP chief political consultant. I have also participated in political rallies, poetry festivals and other cultural events.

3. You had to apply for political asylum on October 15, 1988 after President Cory Aquino cancelled your Philippine passport on September 16, 1988. How did your asylum case proceed and how did it end? Were there offers to grant you political asylum from other countries?

JMS: In 1992, the Raad van State (State Council), the highest administrative court in The Netherlands, recognized me as a political refugee in accordance with the Refugee Convention and ruled further that I could not be deported in accordance with the jurisprudence set in the Soering case, involving the absolute protection under Article 3 of the European Convention on Human Rights. The court even scolded the Dutch justice ministry for having failed to recognize and admit me as a political refugee in four years since my application for political asylum in 1988.

The Dutch justice ministry continued refusing to grant me legal admission as a political refugee despite the ruling of the court that recognized me as a political refugee and the normal practice that such recognition automatically results in legal admission, permanent residence and the choice of the recognized refugee to become even a naturalized citizen in order to normalize his life.

The Dutch Aliens Law was revised to create an Asylum Court system on top of which was the Rechtseenheidskamer (REK – Law Unification Chamber) to which the Justice ministry in 1996 priorly conceded that I was indeed a recognized political refugee under the Geneva Convention and was further protected by Article 3 of the European Convention on Human Rights but argued that it was the freedom of policy of the Dutch state to deny me legal admission and legal residence. The REK ruling upheld the argument of the Dutch justice ministry in 1997. Thus, I have come to be known as the refugee that has actually landed and stayed in The Netherlands but at the same time I am a refugee legally in orbit.

That was the end of my asylum case. But I continued to receive social benefits as asylum seeker until the "terrorist" listing in 2002 that further prompted the Dutch government to end my social benefits. The

US government and the Philippine government had obviously pushed the Dutch government to make life difficult for me in The Netherlands. But I fought back legally and enjoyed the support of the Dutch and other peoples.

No other country offered to grant me political asylum. Within Europe, one can apply for asylum only in the country where one first landed. And for me to seek asylum in another country in Europe or in another continent, would have put me at risk of being apprehended in a third country and deported straight to the Philippines.

4. What happened to the subversion case that the military under Aquino filed against you in Manila in 1988, which prompted her to cancel your passport?

JMS: The subversion case that the military filed against me on September 15, 1988 in order to justify the cancellation of my passport by Cory Aquino became invalidated by President Ramos' repeal of the Anti-Subversion Law in 1992. Ramos also amnestied both the political prisoners and the military mutineers. In the case of the latter, he was completing the process of carrying out the so-called Armacost formula of 1984, which allowed the split in the reactionary armed forces from 1985 to 1986 to allow the downfall of Marcos in 1986 and subsequently to reconcile the factions in the AFP under a new president as commander-in-chief.

Ramos also tried to use the release of political prisoners as a good will measure or incentive for the peace negotiations between the GRP and the NDFP and even as an argument to the Dutch government that I faced no threat of arrest and that I could return to the Philippines freely and without fear.

But in fact the Ramos regime made rebellion a nonbailable capital offense subject to 40 years of imprisonment. This runs counter to the jurisprudence established in the Hernandez rebellion case in 1956, when the Philippine Supreme Court ruled that rebellion was a socially-rooted political offense. Thus it should not be complexed or mixed with common crimes and it is understandably punishable by six to 12 years of imprisonment. The continued deterioration of the legal system is part of the persistent political persecution of persons like me in the Philippines and the anti-democratic decomposition of the Philippine ruling system.

5. While abroad, you were quite successful in pursuing your human rights case against Marcos in the US. How did you do it?

JMS: Indeed, together with 9500 other complainants, I was successful in pursuing the human rights case against Marcos in the US legal system. We availed of a US law that allowed the filing of such a case against a foreigner who resides in the US and has committed human rights violations in his country of origin.

We were after the documentation and court judgment of the human rights violations against us who were victims of illegal detention, torture, disappearances and murder under the Marcos fascist regime, especially because it was impossible to obtain justice in the Philippines against Marcos, the military and the police. The matter of compensation was secondary to proving the culpability of Marcos and his military accomplices for human rights violations.

In the particular case of myself, my wife and my disappeared brother Francisco, Robert Swift the lead lawyer of the complainants did not want us to be among the complainants because of the fear that we would be turnoffs in the US legal system. But the American Civil Liberties Union of Southern California approached my brother Dr. Ramon C. Sison and took up our cases. The Human Rights Watch and the Public Interest Law Center helped us win the case.

My testimony was highly important in the liability phase of the case because I was the only victim of torture to whom Marcos talked before being tortured by his military minions. My deposition was made in Utrecht through the examination by my lead lawyer Paul Hoffman of the ACLU and cross examination by the Marcos lawyer James Lynn. My testimony was recorded by a court stenographer appointed by the district court of Hawaii and was also video-recorded for the Court by a major Dutch video-recording company hired for the purpose.

At first Judge Villareal who heard the case against Marcos kicked me out of the compensation phase of the case because of the false argument that my lawyer did not provide evidence in my favor for that phase. But my evidence had been submitted during the liability phase. I had to appeal to the US Ninth Circuit Court to overrule Villareal. I won the case on appeal and Villareal was compelled to confirm me as one of the winners in the human rights case against Marcos.

My lawyer Paul Hoffman is an outstanding human rights lawyer, having served as legal director of the ACLU Foundation of Southern California and chairman of the Amnesty International. He was assisted by the outstanding Filipino human rights lawyer Atty. Romeo Capulong, founder of the Public Interest Law Center (PILC). The PILC and SELDA (Samahan ng mga Ex-Detainees Laban sa Detensyon at Aresto) were effective in gathering information and public support for the benefit of the victims of human rights violations, including me, Julie and my brother Francisco.

6. You have already received compensation for the torture and detention that you suffered. Does this improve your living condition?

JMS: The compensation of 1.2 million Philippine pesos has been awarded by the Human Rights Claims Board created by the Philippine Congress. This allows me to pay my debts and give a donation to a human rights organization that has been providing me with legal assistance. The amount that remains is just enough to improve my diet and take care of a part of my medical needs.

I do not have enough even to give as token gifts (*balato*) to my children who suffered with me as they were keenly aware of my arrest, torture and illegal detention. But in the first place, they have ample incomes from their own jobs and do not expect any financial gift or assistance from me. I mention my children to stress the limits of my windfall.

7. If any, what legal or political actions were undertaken against you during the time of President Fidel Ramos? It seems that Ramos was more interested in attracting you to the peace negotiations than in pursuing old charges against you or to filing new ones. What happened to the subversion charge filed against you by the Aquino administration and the charge of multiple murder arising from the Plaza Miranda grenade-throwing incident in August 1971?

JMS: Even during the Ramos regime, the military persisted in filing a case against me for every incident allegedly involving the NPA. But Ramos, in particular, was not interested in pressing any charges or making new charges against me. He was more interested in pursuing the peace negotiations than in pursuing old charges or filing new ones against me. In fact, at one time he ordered the release of Wilma Austria after I told him publicly that she was a major campaigner for the peace negotiations.

During Ramos' time as president, the automatic filing of a case against me for every incident being charged against the NPA stopped and through the representation of my lawyer, Atty Romeo T. Capulong, the office of the chief prosecutor archived all the baseless charges against me.

Most important of all, the secretary of Justice Silvestre Bello III, certified in 1996 that there were no pending charges against me, because earlier in 1992 the subversion case against me had been invalidated by the repeal of the Anti-Subversion Law and the Manila prosecutors office had dismissed as based on pure speculation the false charge of multiple murder arising from the 1971 Plaza Miranda grenade-throwing incident.

8. Did President Estrada take any legal action against you? Or was he more interested in extra-legal action against you? What happened to your complaint against the assassination plot against you?

JMS: Estrada did not take any legal action against me. But he was more interested in extra-legal action against me. This was publicly exposed by Col. Reynaldo Berroya over DZBB radio in January 2001 that military officers under Estrada had plotted my assassination and had sent one hit team after another to The Netherlands in 1999 and 2000.

Upon my request to him, Col. Berroya came over to Utrecht and together with Atty. Romeo T. Capulong we went to the Utrecht police to report the information that we had about the assassination plot against me.

The Dutch prosecution office formally declared to my Dutch lawyer Michiel Pestman that the Dutch police had confirmed the veracity of some of the evidence provided by Berroya and even the passport of one member of the hit team. However under Dutch law, no case could be pursued because the assassination did not occur and it is arguable that the would-be assassins changed their mind. Anyway, the assassination plot had ended with the ouster of Estrada from power through mass protests.

9. In the time of Mrs. Arroyo, several legal or political actions were taken against you in the Philippines and abroad. These included among others the rebellion case involving the alleged Hilongos killings and the terrorist listing by the US and other countries, including The Netherlands. Please explain the circumstances of these actions against you by the US and Dutch governments.

JMS: In Arroyo's time, several legal and political actions were taken against me. I was blamed for every incident charged against the NPA. I was made the principal accused in the so-called Hilongos case or the case of the travelling skeletons. The charge is absurd. I was under maximum security detention and had no position whatsoever in the CPP or the NPA when the alleged murder of several people occurred in Hilongos, Leyte in 1985. I was in no position and in no circumstances to give any order or command for the NPA to do anything.

The most serious legal action taken against me abroad was my being designated as a "terrorist" by the US, followed by the Dutch government and then by the EU in 2002. Then in 2007 the Dutch government acted on the charges originating from the Manila government that I allegedly used Dutch territory to order the NPA to murder several persons in the Philippines. I was arrested on August 27, 2007 and detained in solitary confinement for 17 days.

10. What happened to each case? What were the consequences to you? What did you do to fight back? Who in particular helped you fight back?

JMS: The Supreme Court under Chief Justice Reynato Puno ordered in June 2007 the dismissal of the Hilongos rebellion case as based on rubbish and scolded the prosecution for prostituting the noble profession of prosecution.

My being listed as a terrorist by the Dutch government and then by the EU became the basis for the freezing of my bank account and withdrawal of social benefits which continued even after my winning the case before the European Court of Justice for the removal of my name from the terrorist list.

The false charge of murder in 2007 caused my arrest and detention in solitary confinement for 17 days, which was of course inconvenient and humiliating. The appellate court dismissed the charge in October 2007. The NDF Information Office, my home and six other homes were raided and papers, computers and other paraphernalia were carted away by the police. These were not returned immediately even after the case was dropped and police investigation was stopped in early 2010.

For each case in The Netherlands I had a team of lawyers. In the EU case, against the terrorist listing, my lawyers were led by Jan Fermon. In the case against the false murder charge, my lawyers were led by Michiel Pestman. All my lawyers were outstanding in the fields of international human rights and criminal law. They were assisted by my Filipino lawyers led by Atty. Romeo T. Capulong and Atty. Rachel Pastores of the Public Interest Law Center.

A special committee to defend me politically was formed because of the powerful "anti-terrorist" propaganda from the Rightists in the Philippines, US and The Netherlands. It was steered by Ruth de Leon. It had a website administered by Jan Beentjes. It was composed of representatives of the Filipino community and the European parties and organizations in solidarity with the Filipino people's struggle for national and social liberation. The formations, which were represented in the committee extended to me popular support of incalculable value.

The filmmaker Kor Al and my pro bono Dutch lawyer Bernard E. J. M. Tomlow traveled to the Philippines and made a powerful video, Terror or Arbitrariness, which was broadcast in a major Dutch national TV station. The video featured the Philippine Vice President Teofisto Guingona, House Speaker José de Venecia, Senator Loren Legarda, Bishop Julio Labayen, Philippine Independent Church Supreme Bishop Tomas Millamena, and urban poor leader Ka Mameng Deunida, all highly respected Filipino personages defending me.

11. What legal or political actions were undertaken against you during the time of Aquino III?

JMS: Under the Aquino II regime, the psywar campaign of vilification against me by the military continued, especially after the breakdown of the peace negotiations. I was accused of masterminding every alleged act of the NPA against the reactionary government. But Aquino did not push any legal action to be taken against me in The Netherlands or elsewhere abroad. In this kind of persecutory action, the Arroyo regime did the worst against me, especially because of her rabid anti-communist national security adviser Norberto Gonzales.

12. Duterte is now flinging several charges against you, including the revived Hilongos case and terrorism. Can you explain the content and circumstances of these charges. How do you respond to them?

JMS: The Hilongos case has been revived because the Supreme Court headed by a Duterte presidential flunkey accepted an amendment of the original charge junked by the Supreme Court headed by Puno. This case does not bother me because of the glaring falsity of the claims against me and against my co-accused. But the case is being dragged by the military by listing witnesses that do not even show up and causing long postponements.

What seems to be the more serious legal action of the Duterte regime against me is the attempt of the Manila court to summon me to Manila for interrogation and somehow to use my absence as something in favor of the case to proscribe the CPP and NPA as "terrorist" and thereafter use the judicial proscription to arrest a multitude of people as "terrorist."

I have already issued a statement to the effect that there is no basis for summoning me because it has been established that in the cases of the EU terrorist listing and the multiple murder that I am not an operational leader of the CPP or the NPA. It is also clear that I cannot be compelled to go to Manila because I am protected by the Refugee Convention and by Article 3 of the European Convention on Human Rights.

Chapter VII

On and off peace negotiations

1. Did the CPP and the NDFP have a framework before actually engaging in peace negotiations?

JMS: The CPP and the NDFP have a framework before actively engaging in peace negotiations. You can review the full exposition of this framework by reading the two articles on "The People's Struggle for a Just Peace" in my book, *For Justice, Socialism and Peace*. The titles of the two articles are self-explanatory: "History and Circumstances Relevant to the Question of Peace" and "The NDFP Framework in Contrast to the GRP Framework."

Despite the conflicting GRP and NDFP frameworks, especially at their maximum levels, their respective representatives were able to establish a common framework for peace negotiations in "The Hague Joint Declaration" of September 1, 1992. The essence of the framework is to hold peace negotiations in order to address the roots of the armed conflict and to agree on social and economic as well as political and constitutional reforms to lay the basis for a just and lasting peace.

The peace negotiations are to be guided by mutually acceptable principles such as national sovereignty, democracy and social justice; and no precondition shall be made to negate the inherent character and purpose of peace negotiations.

2. Did Marcos ever offer peace negotiations to the revolutionary movement? When you were in prison, were you ever approached on that matter?

JMS: Soon after I was arrested on November 10, 1977, I was brought by my temporary constabulary custodians to Marcos at close to noontime and he himself offered peace negotiations for national unity and reconciliation. I said that it was possible but that I was not in any position to negotiate because I was a captive. I also said that I could only help in preparing for the negotiations between representatives of the revolutionary movement and the government.

Marcos came to the point of offering peace negotiations by saying that he had read my writings. He also mentioned that supposed friends of mine, like Blas Ople, Adrian Cristobal and Andres Cristobal Cruz, had joined his government. They were his "nationalist" ghost writers. There was a basis for Marcos to sound friendly because I once met him in the presidential palace in 1966 when he invited the National Council of the Movement for the Advancement of Nationalism (MAN) to meet with him. I was then the General Secretary of MAN and Sen. Lorenzo Tañada was the Chairman.

But he and the military were more interested in torturing me first and ferreting out information from me regarding the identity of my successor in the CPP Central Committee and in locations of the CPP central offices. But I was able to withstand the torture without giving any information damaging to any comrade, friend or ally. And the torture served to stress the point in my mind that I was in the den of the monsters.

In 1981, Marcos used a high military intelligence officer to try to solicit my help in sending word to the CPP to open up for peace negotiations. But I hedged and evaded the solicitation. From that time onwards, I did not hear from Marcos about peace negotiations again.

3. What was the nature of the negotiations in 1986 between the NDFP and the Manila government? What did it lead to after the ceasefire agreement was signed on November 22, 1986?

JMS: The negotiations in 1986 between the GRP under Aquino and the NDFP was basically about ceasefire between the armed forces of the two sides, with the objective of using the period of ceasefire as the occasion for the GRP and the NDFP negotiating panels to agree on the agenda of the prospective peace negotiations.

Thus, a 60-day ceasefire agreement was signed on November 22, 1986. The ceasefire agreement was disrupted on January 22, 1987 when the presidential guards and other reinforcing military forces assaulted the peaceful demonstration of mostly peasants and their urban supporters demanding genuine land reform. They massacred thirteen and injured hundreds more peasant activists and sympathizers. This is now known historically as the 1987 Mendiola massacre.

Instead of holding the military officers responsible and ordering their investigation and prosecution, Aquino absolved them and "unsheathed" her "sword of war" against the NDFP, the revolutionary movement and the national democratic mass movement and terminated the ceasefire agreement on February 7, 1987. NDFP personnel exposed to enemy surveillance in the course of the ceasefire negotiations in Manila but who could not promptly go underground, were subjected to arrest, torture, indefinite detention and summary executions. Thus Aquino incited the people and the revolutionary forces to intensify the armed revolution.

4. As early as 1989 Mrs. Aquino approached the NDFP for exploration of peace negotiations. Rep. José V. Yap was sent to the Netherlands to offer such negotiations. Henceforth, what followed?

JMS: When Mrs. Aquino was being threatened with a military coup, she sent Rep. José Yap to The Netherlands to find out from me and Luis Jalandoni, NDFP chief international representative, whether the NDFP would be interested in peace negotiations. We said that we were open to the possibility, provided the peace negotiations would be held in a foreign neutral venue because of the bitter experiences suffered by NDFP personnel who were arrested or killed after Aquino unsheathed the sword of war in February 1987.

Rep. Yap came twice for exploratory discussions. We were ready to start the peace process when the Noble military mutiny occurred in Mindanao in December 1990. The mutiny had the effect of frightening Aquino from pursuing peace negotiations. She overestimated the adverse consequences of the mutiny to her and she became too terrified to engage in peace negotiations with the NDFP. From then on, she stopped sending Rep. Yap to The Netherlands.

5. When did the peace negotiations really start? Did they not start in 1992, with the signing of The Hague Joint Declaration as the framework agreement? What were the main contents?

JMS: The preliminary peace talks started when the representatives of the GRP headed by Rep. José Yap and those of the NDFP headed by Luis Jalandoni met to forge The Hague Joint Declaration in 1992. At that time, Ramos was already the president.

Yap was in a position to serve as chief negotiator because he had been a long time friend of the NDFP and had already done exploratory talks during the time of Aquino. It was quite ironic that during the time of Aquino, Ramos as defense secretary had set unacceptable preconditions like not releasing political prisoners who had belonged to the NPA and insisting on the Philippines as venue for the peace negotiations.

The main contents of The Hague Joint Declaration are as follows:

1. Formal peace negotiations shall be held to resolve the armed conflict;
2. The common goal of the aforesaid negotiations shall be the attainment of a just and lasting peace;
3. Such negotiations shall take place after the parties have reached tentative agreement on substantive issues in the agreed agenda through the reciprocal working committees to be separately organized by the GRP and the NDFP;
4. The holding of peace negotiations must be in accordance with mutually acceptable principles, including national sovereignty, democracy and social justice and no precondition shall be made to negate the inherent character and purpose of the peace negotiations; and
5. Preparatory to the formal peace negotiations, we [the GRP and NDFP] have agreed to recommend the following:
   a. Specific measures of goodwill and confidence building to create a favorable climate for peace negotiations; and
   b. The substantive agenda of the formal peace negotiations shall include human rights and international humanitarian law, socioeconomic reforms, political and constitutional reforms, end of hostilities and disposition of forces.

6. What happened after the signing of The Hague Joint Declaration during the entire term of the Ramos administration? What was finally accomplished? Why could not a final peace agreement be reached then?

JMS: After the GRP and the NDFP negotiating panels signed The Hague Joint Declaration, the peace process could not proceed further because the following day Ramos created the National Unification Commission (NUC) headed by Haydee Yorac to pursue so-called localized peace talks.

The NDFP denounced the creation and work of NUC as running counter to the peace negotiations already agreed upon in The Hague Joint Declaration. Speaker De Venecia and Rep. Yap persuaded Ramos in 1993 to dissolve the NUC and give way to the GRP-NDFP peace negotiations. Then the representatives of the two sides came together in a series of meetings to forge the Joint Agreement on Safety and Immunity Guarantees (JASIG) and the Ground Rules of Meetings in February 1995.

After these agreements were signed, the GRP and the NDFP negotiating panels were ready to open the formal peace negotiations in ceremonies in Brussels, Belgium in June 1995. The formal opening was indeed made and the panels signed the Joint Agreement on the Sequence, Formation and Operationalization of the Reciprocal Working Committees. But the NDFP warned that it would not engage in further meetings unless NDFP peace consultant Sotero Llamas was released from prison as the GRP had promised even before the formal opening. The formal talks could not be resumed for several months until Llamas was released.

During the Ramos regime, the negotiating panels succeeded in hammering out a total of ten major agreements, including the Comprehensive Agreement on Respect for Human Rights and International Humanitarian Law (CARHRIHL), the first item in the substantive agenda of the peace negotiations.

During Ramos' term, there was enough time to reach a final peace agreement. But the delays in the formal talks were caused by key military officers, especially Defense Secretary Renato de Villa, who insisted on detaining Llamas.

7. Initially, Mr. Estrada made a positive step in the peace negotiations by approving the Comprehensive Agreement on Respect for Human Rights and International Humanitarian Law (CARHRIHL), which Ramos did not sign. What eventually made Estrada change his mind?

JMS: In the first year, it looked like Estrada would agree to the acceleration of the peace process, especially because he signed the CARHRIHL, which Ramos had not signed before the end of his term. But he was insecure in his position as commander-in-chief and tended to follow the advice of ultra-reactionary military officers who wanted a protracted indefinite ceasefire while the peace negotiations were going on.

His susceptibility to the worst advice or intrigue of his military advisers and his own temperament as some kind of a braggart and goon manifested itself when he unnecessarily terminated the peace negotiations on May 31, 1999 as a reaction to the NPA's capture of

Brigadier General Victor Obillo and his military aide Capt. Eduardo Montealto in Mindanao and to the NDFP position against his approval of the Visiting Forces Agreement with the US.

The CPP and the NDF had already announced that they were ready to release General Obillo and his military aide if the AFP would issue an order for the Suspension of Military Operations (SOMO) in the pertinent area for the safe and orderly release of the two POWs. But Estrada preferred to use the capture of Brigadier General Obillo and Capt. Montealto as pretext for terminating the peace negotiations.

The same impulsiveness and rashness under the pressure of his own military subordinates were evident in his abrupt order to attack Camp Abubakar, the main Moro Islamic Liberation Front (MILF) camp. This broke the ceasefire agreement with the MILF and ignited a long sustained war, upsetting the precarious budget of the reactionary government.

8. How were the peace negotiations resumed under the Arroyo administration? What were the positive developments and how and why did the negotiations head for the rocks under her and the following administration of Benigno Aquino III ?

JMS: Mrs. Arroyo was to a great extent grateful to the national democratic movement, especially to the workers and youth of the national democratic movement for having organized the mass protest actions that effected the ouster of Estrada and her succession to the presidency. She proceeded to order the arrest of Estrada in order to stop him from reclaiming his office.

As soon as she took office, she sent Rep. Hernani Braganza to Utrecht to pave the way for the resumption of the peace negotiations. The GRP and the NDFP agreed to avail of the Royal Norwegian government as the third party facilitator. To prevail over the termination of the peace negotiations, the GRP and the NDFP negotiating panels simply reaffirmed all the agreements since The Hague Joint Declaration of 1992.

They approved the Operating Guidelines of the Joint Monitoring Committee in order to implement provisions of the CARHRIHL to receive complaints of violations of human rights and international humanitarian law and advice the party concerned to act on the complaints from the other side.

The Arroyo regime "suspended" the peace negotiations when reactionary military officers demanded this in reaction to the death of a notorious human rights violator, Cagayan governor and former military colonel Rodolfo Aguinaldo as he resisted his arrest by an NPA unit. The regime used this killing as the pretext for ending the peace negotiations because of its failure to make the NDFP agree to a protracted and indefinite ceasefire agreement.

Peace negotiations were resumed during the time of Benigno Aquino III. They were at first promising because his negotiators were known to be patriotic and progressive but the head of Office of the Presidential Adviser on the Peace Process (OPAPP), Teresita Deles, was a notorious anticommunist and social-democrat of the ultra-Right kind.

When the most reactionary military officers in the Aquino II regime could not get the protracted ceasefire agreement to paralyze the NPA, they decided to sabotage the peace negotiations by merely using incidents of military encounter with the NPA as the pretext for scuttling the peace negotiations.

9. At first, Mr. Duterte seemed eager to resume the peace negotiations and he even promised amnesty and release of all political prisoners. How come the pendulum instead swung to the extreme right, while in late 2018 he declared to put up his own "Duterte Death Squad" (DDS) to hunt down the NPA as well as the legal left, all of whom he suddenly tagged as "terrorists"?

JMS: Before the May 2016 elections, as early as 2014, Duterte made big promises like forming a coalition government with the CPP, releasing all political prisoners and carrying out social, economic and political reforms. On May 16, 2016, a week after his election as president, Duterte promised to the NDFP emissary Fidel Agcaoili before witnesses that he would amnesty and release all political prisoners. But as soon as he assumed the presidency, he declared that he would not fulfil his promise to amnesty and release all political prisoners.

From the very beginning of his presidency, Duterte launched an all-out war against the NPA under the guise of continuing his predecessor's Oplan Bayanihan until he launched his own Oplan Kapayapaan (Peace) in January 2017. He pretended to be for peace negotiations from the beginning of his term until May 23, 2007 when he proclaimed martial law in Mindanao against the Bangsamoro and the Filipino people.

He himself was intensifying the military offensives against the NPA and the communities suspected of supporting the NPA even during the long ceasefire from August 2016 to February 2017. The NPA units adhered to the ceasefire and evaded the enemy offensives. But every time the NPA had to take self-defense action, Duterte heaped verbal abuse on the NPA and declared to the media one termination of the formal talks after another.

Eventually, Duterte issued Proclamation 360 on November 23, 2017 in order to terminate the peace negotiations and then Proclamation 374 on December 5, 2017 designating the CPP and NPA as "terrorist." He deliberately and wrongfully declared the JASIG invalid and inoperative, despite its provisions that protect all NDFP and GRP negotiators and related personnel in case of termination or breakdown of peace negotiations.

While the NDFP has strictly followed these provisions in favor the GRP negotiating and related personnel, Duterte has ordered his armed agents to arrest and even kill on sight NDFP negotiators and consultants if there were no hostile witnesses to the murder. Such was the fate of NDFP peace consultant Randy Felix Malayao who was murdered on January 31, 2019 by a Duterte death squad while sleeping in a bus without any companions.

The method of mass murder in Oplan Tokhang (short of toktok hangyo, meaning knock and plead) in the pseudo-war on drugs are now being applied on a wide scale to social activists and Duterte critics. These are tagged as "communist terrorists" and become open prey to the death squads who get paid for every murder they commit.

The Duterte regime is now in the process of obtaining a pro forma court approval for the proscription of the CPP and the NDFP as "terrorist" in order subsequently to list individuals and organizations as part of the CPP and the NPA and therefore as "terrorist" and subject to punitive actions by official military and police units as well as by their shadowy death squads. The mass murder of social activists and critics of the regime has already started in earnest in rural and urban-poor areas since the second half of 2017.

10. Did Duterte deliberately foul up the peace negotiations with his repeated terminations and then finally terminating them through Proclamation 360?

JMS: The tyrant Duterte has deliberately fouled up and terminated the peace negotiations with Proclamation 360 to practically use the continuing armed conflict as the pretext for an iron-fisted and bloody presidency and to carry out a proclaimed or de facto martial law nationwide. He has practically imposed a regime of open terror on the Filipino people. This directly related to the establishment of a fascist dictatorship through charter change to a bogus kind of federalism.

It is of decisive importance to Duterte that he keeps the peace negotiations terminated so that he can proceed either to declare nationwide martial law formally or realize a de facto kind of martial law that uses his "anti-terrorist" Proclamation 374 to run down all kinds of opposition, whether these are suspected revolutionaries or intrasystemic opposition or critics, by simply red-tagging them and unleashing a wide range of punitive measures, including assassinations by death squads.

11. Is there any hope for resuming such negotiations given the fact that several NDFP consultants have been (re)arrested and even killed? Do you anticipate an ever escalating civil war?

JMS: The chances for the resumption of peace negotiations are very slim or absent. Duterte has done everything to terminate the peace negotiations and to prevent their resumption. He has thoroughly violated the JASIG and has ordered his armed minions to arrest or kill (in the absence of witnesses unbeholden to the regime) NDFP negotiators and consultants. Therefore, the revolutionary movement has no choice but to defend itself and intensify the people's struggle in order to weaken and isolate the tyrannical Duterte regime and thereby support the movement to oust this regime.

The slim chance for the resumption of peace negotiations with the Duterte regime depends on how Duterte reacts to the failure of his all-out war and the advance of the armed revolution. One possible reaction is for him to escalate state terrorism and the other is to sue for peace and engage in peace negotiations. Otherwise, the resumption of peace negotiations will have to take place after Duterte is either ousted, finishes his term in 2022 or succumbs to illness, whose gravity is publicly indicated by the chronic discoloration of his face, his wobbly walk and senseless rants.

12. Will Mr. Duterte's offer of localized peace talks and of bounties for those who surrender prove effective?

JMS: Duterte's so-called localized peace talks are a charade. His armed minions stage them by using local officials to gather the people to meetings where they are told to sign an attendance sheet and raise their hands for photographing sessions whereafter they are misrepresented to the press as NPA surrenderers. It is absurd that there are now several times more NPA surrenderers than the PNP- and AFP-estimated 4,000 NPA fighters. Thereby the regime unwittingly exposes its own lies.

Corruption is involved in such gatherings of fake surrender. The military and police officers pocket the supposed cash awards to fake surrenderers. Worst of all, the fake lists of surrenderers are used as basis for military and police officers to commit murders because of higher cash rewards for fake NPA casualties.

The cash rewards for the military officers in Oplan Kapayapaan are further criminalizing and corrupting the reactionary armed forces just as the police officers have been criminalized and corrupted by cash rewards for the murder of suspected drug users and peddlers in urban poor communities.

There are practically no genuine NPA surrenderers. A big number of poseurs are long time assets of the reactionaries and misrepresented as NPA surrenderers. Only a few suspected NPA fighters are actually arrested and then persuaded to pose as surrenderers in exchange for cash awards in order to give a semblance of reality to the surrender program under the false claim of localized peace talks.

Chapter VIII

Prospects of the Philippine revolution

1. What is the basis for the expectation of the revolutionary movement to advance and prevail against the ruling system?

JMS: The chronic crisis of the semicolonial and semifeudal ruling system continues to worsen. The Philippine ruling system is on an irreversible course of decomposition. It is heading for a revolutionary overthrow as desired by the people. The only way to delay the momentum of the revolutionary movement is for the exploiting classes of big compradors, landlords and bureaucrat capitalists to allow the peace process to succeed and give way to the demands for national sovereignty, democratic empowerment of the people, social justice, expanded social services and economic development through national industrialization and land reform.

But it is difficult to expect the exploiting classes to agree even only to substantive bourgeois democratic reforms that would result in the development of the country. The overthrow of the Marcos fascist dictatorship was followed by a series of pseudo-democratic and fundamentally counterrevolutionary regimes. And now, the people are faced with a new tyrannical regime hell-bent on imposing a full-blown fascist dictatorship. They are driven by their oppression and exploitation to wage the just struggle for new democratic revolution.

We expect that the conditions for waging revolution will become more favorable from year to year; and from decade to decade. The global scourge of neoliberalism, the frequent economic and political crises, state terrorism and the wars of aggression unleashed by US imperialism and the reactionary forces will give rise to unprecedentedly intense and widespread armed revolutions for national liberation, democracy and socialism. We are on the eve of the resurgence of revolutionary struggles on a global scale.

2. Why has the call for maturing the stage of the strategic defensive and moving forward to the stage of strategic stalemate been repeatedly made but the struggle is still snagged on the stage of strategic defensive?

JMS: For the people's democratic revolution in the Philippines to achieve total victory, the protracted people's war has to pass through the probable stages of strategic defensive, strategic stalemate and the strategic offensive. The armed revolution can only achieve total victory by completing the defensive stage, proceeding to the strategic stalemate and moving faster toward the strategic offensive. From one stage to the other, the growth of the people's army is cumulative. We can therefore expect that the strategic stalemate would take a shorter time to run and reach the strategic offensive.

A number of times, the CPP leadership has called for the completion of the strategic defensive and the advance to the strategic stalemate. But each time there is a snag. First, the snag was "Left" opportunism from 1981 to 1991 reducing the rate of advance.

Now the problem is conservatism, which ran for some decades to reduce the rate of advance in the people's war. But this is now being solved. The revolutionary forces and the people are confident that the current rectification movement and the intensification of the people's war can certainly pave the way to the strategic stalemate, as a necessary stage before the strategic offensive.

We must also take into account international factors. It is not only the revisionist betrayal of socialism and the full restoration of capitalism in revisionist-ruled countries that have had an adverse impact on the Philippine revolution. But more importantly, the neoliberal policy regime has been able to manipulate finance capital in order to buoy up the global and national economies from one round of crisis to another, further deepening but covering up the crisis. After four decades, neoliberalism has become completely unsustainable. A bigger bubble, the global debt burden, is already in the process of bursting.

3. What are the factors and conditions for advancing the revolution? Don't you see the dangers of a war of attrition dragging on for quite some time?

JMS: The subjective factors of the people's democratic revolution are the revolutionary party of the proletariat as the leading force, the peasant movement as the main force and base of the people's army, the revolutionary mass organizations, the united front and the people's democratic government.

Those who complain that the people's democratic revolution has taken too long think only in terms of being able to seize the presidential palace in Manila in order to measure success. They fail to recognize that together with other revolutionary forces, the people's democratic government has been established and is gaining ground and developing in the countryside from the village level to higher levels of administration.

At the height of his rampage in destroying Marawi City, Duterte made himself look like a clown to the NPA by taunting the revolutionary fighters for supposedly not being able to occupy and defend a single village unlike the Maute group, which was making a decisive engagement in Marawi City. The NPA does not have that foolish or putschist kind of strategy. It fights only the battles that it can win on the ground it chooses because it is favorable to it. The seizure of Malacañang will come after the revolutionary movement and government have advanced wave upon wave from their bastions in the countryside in a protracted people's war.

The objective conditions favorable to the subjective forces of the revolution are growing. They are the worsening crisis of the ruling system, the intensifying contradictions among the factions of the exploiting classes, the rising anti-imperialist movement and class struggle, the strategic decline of US imperialism and the intensifying contradictions among the imperialist powers, resulting in trade wars and wars of aggression.

The people's war in the Philippines has already protracted for more than 50 years. Consequently, it is gentle in comparison to other armed revolutions. The oft-repeated estimate of 40,000 casualties is divisible between some 10,000 enemy troops killed in battle by the NPA, and 30,000 mostly civilians indiscriminately killed by the reactionary military and police in acts of revenge after battles won by the NPA.

Attrition is mainly at the expense of the enemy not only in terms of casualties but also in terms of military equipment, vehicles, depots and other structures destroyed by the NPA. The enemy is spending billions just to maintain personnel and operations, and provide supplies to them. The costs of the armed counterrevolution and the corruption that goes with them are weakening the reactionary state to the very core.

While the people's war is protracted, the CPP, NPA and NDFP, the mass organizations and the people's democratic government are gaining ground and strength. They use time to develop their strength in stages in every part of the Philippines. Their objective is to accelerate the advance of the armed revolution but they cannot outstrip what the subjective factors and objective conditions permit.

Thus, they say that they will keep on fighting for as long as necessary, even as long as Dagohoy whose tribe in Bohol fought the Spanish colonialists for 80 years or the more than 300 years of intermittent uprisings against Spanish colonialism until the Filipino nation achieved victory in 1898.

4. Is it possible for the people's democratic revolution to win mainly or solely on the basis of the "deterioration" of the domestic ruling system?

JMS: It is not possible for the people's democratic revolution to win mainly or solely on the basis of the deterioration of the ruling system. The revolutionary forces have to grow in strength and advance with the correct line, avoid committing major and minor mistakes and correct mistakes promptly through criticism and self-criticism and rectification campaigns as the case may be, depending on the gravity of the mistakes.

The revolutionaries can be confident of victory so long as they uphold the correct general line, which is the people's democratic revolution in the Philippines, to confront, fight and defeat the semicolonial and semifeudal ruling system. Friends and enemies are identified in class terms. The stages and phases of the revolution are well understood and the long-term perspective of socialism is guaranteed by the effective leadership of the working class and its revolutionary party.

The rate of advance of the Philippine revolution can be reduced by conditions external to the domestic ruling system. In the 1960s until 1975, the focus of the world revolution was in Southeast Asia, especially Vietnam and the rest of Indochina. But since then, the chain of neocolonialism in the underdeveloped countries, revisionism in socialist counties and neoliberalism in the entire world has served to counter the trend of the anti-imperialist movement and the world proletarian revolution.

But the Philippine revolution has withstood the attacks by the Marcos fascist dictatorship and the adverse effects of counterrevolutionary developments abroad. Under the most adverse and threatening conditions, the Philippine revolutionary movement has prevailed and stood out as a torch bearer of the anti-imperialist movement and the world proletarian revolution in the same manner that the old democratic revolution of 1896 became the torch bearer for the later bourgeois democratic revolutions in Asia.

5. Can you describe the rate and scope at which the ruling system in the Philippines is "deteriorating" and how do you gauge that?

JMS: The economy remains underdeveloped, agrarian, pre-industrial and semifeudal. It is dominated by a combination of the comprador big bourgeoisie and landlord class, with the former dominant in the cities and the latter in the countryside. Between the two, the comprador big bourgeoisie is wealthier and more powerful and has landed estates of its own. It is the principal ruling class in the semifeudal economy, in contrast to bygone feudal times before the middle of the 19th century when the landlord class was the principal exploiting class.

In the current period of the neoliberal policy regime, the comprador big bourgeoisie is the principal trading and financial agent of foreign monopoly capitalism in running and distorting the economy. Agricultural production for domestic consumption has drastically gone down, ironically in an agrarian country. Grain and other staple food imports have risen.

Import-dependent manufacturing and semi-manufacturing for re-export have gone down since the Asian financial crisis. Export-oriented logging, plantations and mining have continued with their production understated and undervalued for the purpose of evading taxes. Their exports are increasingly underpriced and their products are diverted from local processing.

The glossy part of the economy includes the periods of boom in the private construction of high rise office, hotel and residential buildings and shopping malls and the flagrant display of luxury imports by the exploiting classes and their highly paid professionals, with their high level of import-dependent consumption, which go with the rising government expenditures of the most corrupt and parasitic kind to bloat the GDP.

The investment part of the GDP has been accounted for mainly by extractive, finance, trading and service enterprises that have nothing to do with industrial development. Nonproductive portfolio investments from foreign hedge funds dramatically buoyed up the economy during the Aquino regime but are now flowing out to seek higher interest rates elsewhere.

The grossly unequal trade perpetuates control by imperialist powers and its big comprador agents over the country's supply of raw mineral and agricultural products for export. While these are undervalued, manufactured imports for consumption and semi-manufacturing are overvalued. Thus, the perennial and growing trade deficit that requires more foreign borrowing and greater dependence on the export of cheap labor. The imperialist plunder in the economic and trade pattern blocks genuine national industrialization and results in massive poverty, unemployment and inhuman conditions of employment in both urban and rural areas.

The neocolonial extraction of raw materials has resulted in massive deforestation, loss of ground water, irrigation and drinking water crises, loss of organic matter, soil erosion, silting and pollution of rivers, lakes, coral reefs, dams and canals, flooding, landslides, hotter and drier micro-climates, droughts, lower harvests and fish catch, loss of pollination agents, massive extinction of species, and loss of biodiversity, including potential life-saving medicine.

Rather than have nationally-owned-and-controlled industries employing more people and paying adequate wages, the Philippine economy is made to host the mere assembly of semiconductors from imported and consigned manufactured parts by imperialist firms and using workers paid less than half of the minimum decent cost of living. Employment opportunities for college graduates have been mostly narrowed to jobs in call centers, which serve the back-office needs of imperialist corporations in the US and elsewhere. Those employed get far lower wages than workers in capitalist countries.

The centerpiece "Build, Build, Build" infrastructure program of the Duterte regime is aimed at speeding up the transport, flow and movements in the lopsided and neocolonial trade. But it will put the Philippines in the debt trap of China and other imperialist countries, as the foreign loans are used to pay for overpriced imported construction and engineering equipment, building materials and all sorts of services. The costs of the program will gobble up taxpayer money and cause severe trade and budgetary deficits.

The economy is made extremely dependent on foreign loans and the foreign exchange earnings of overseas contract workers to cover the growing trade and budgetary deficits. The persistent depression and stagnation of the global economy and the rising tide against migrant workers threaten to cut down the foreign exchange remittances of

Filipino migrant workers. The US Federal Reserve System has also started to raise interest rates, which is resulting in the tightening of international credit for the Philippines.

Meanwhile, feudal tenancy or sharecropping remains widespread. More than 90 percent of so-called reform beneficiaries are unable to keep up with the yearly land amortizations to the government's bogus land reform program. But even those able to do so eventually are forced by the underpricing of their produce to mortgage their land-holdings to moneylenders, who now become their new landlords and rent-collectors. At the same time, trader cartels continue to manipulate and drive down farmgate prices.

Keeping farmgate prices even more depressed has been the rice import liberalization policy of the Duterte government, which authorizes unlimited importation of rice by the same rice cartels. Instead of providing adequate coverage and funding of just farmgate price support for peasants' local-food produce as part and parcel of a genuine land reform program, the reactionary government has slavishly obeyed the neoliberal dictates of the IMF and imperialist banks to fully disable rather than reinforce the National Food Authority and give free rein to private agricultural cartels.

Massive imports of rice and vegetables are sending already far depressed farmgate prices even lower, deepening poverty even more in the countryside. Compounding the semifeudal plight of rice farmers and other peasants is the overpriced cost of imported inputs like agrochemicals and invasive hybrid seeds, for which they are forced to borrow from usurers. This trade not only cuts down their farm incomes but also poisons the aquifers and wells, and acidifies the soil, robbing it and the crops themselves of vital nutrients.

The exploiting classes and the reactionary government are systematically increasing land monopoly and concentration in the interest both of export-oriented plantations and real estate speculation in the upper middle class housing and tourist facilities. In the process, this trend is drastically reducing the amount of land that is promised and available for land reform. The land frontier for spontaneous resettlement of the surplus rural population has been gone since 1969. It has been taken over by bureaucrat capitalists, big comprador landlords and foreign capitalists in logging, mining and plantations.

The poor peasants and farm workers are left with scarce or no income at all and an increasing number of them flock to urban areas seeking odd jobs and commingling with the mostly underemployed and unemployed workers and semiproletariat engaged in all sorts of low-income artisanal work and other odd jobs. These are highly combustible conditions for revolution in the countryside as well as in urban poor communities. The revolutionary forces can recruit members and develop cadres from among the unemployed, underemployed and those who live on subhuman levels of income.

The dire conditions of the exploited and impoverished workers and peasants are in sharp contradiction to the atrociously high incomes of foreign and big comprador corporations, the exploiting classes and the corrupt bureaucrats. Under these conditions, there is ample basis for the anti-imperialist and class struggle to grow and advance. It is only a matter of the revolutionary forces becoming more effective in arousing, organizing and mobilizing the oppressed and exploited people. Meanwhile, the unjust character of the ruling system is also being increasingly exposed by the spiraling virulence and violence of the conflicts among the political factions of the exploiting classes.

6. It is predictable or even obvious now that the imperialist powers compete in enlarging their respective interests in the Philippines. But they can agree on suppressing the Philippine revolution. Which imperialist powers are most likely to engage in military intervention in the Philippines, apart from the US currently?

JMS: The imperialist powers that are already most engaged in economic competition and political rivalry over the Philippines are the US and China. It is worth watching how they carry out their trade war, despite their deep background in being the main partners in so-called neoliberal globalization, especially in the Philippines, and how they compete in making investments and supplying arms that the Duterte regime asks for.

Duterte previously claimed that he was pursuing an independent foreign policy and was countervailing the prior overall US dominance with closer Philippine relations with China. But the fact has become conspicuous that the US retains supreme dominance over the Philippines in an all-round way while Duterte is falling for China's tricks to make the Philippines a Chinese debt colony with the use of high interest loans for overpriced infrastructure projects. China is also pressuring Duterte to explicitly give up Philippine sovereign rights over the West

Philippine Sea and the rich undersea mineral (especially oil and gas) and marine resources.

In the face of the rising armed revolution in the Philippines, the two imperialist powers most likely to intervene militarily are the US and China. The reactionary government will beg for more foreign military assistance, including increased foreign advisors and troops, as was demonstrated in the destruction of Marawi City. The US provided the drones for surveillance and the planes and bombs for destroying the city in collaboration with Filipino-piloted planes. China supplied infantry-type firearms.

There may be occasions in the future when the US and China, together with their respective partners, are provided with areas for occupation in case of aggression meant to combat the NPA during the strategic stalemate or strategic offensive and prevent or delay total victory of the armed revolution. Under the Enhanced Defense Cooperation Agreement (EDCA), the US military forces maintain and operate their own bases within major camps of the reactionary armed forces.

For its part, the Chinese have militarized the artificial islands they built in the West Philippine Sea and will certainly demand that they be allowed to provide and field their own security forces for the protection of Chinese projects and personnel in the Philippines. However, we cannot say fully how fast and how far the collaboration or contention between the US and China would evolve.

7. How do you counteract the possibilities of foreign military intervention?

JMS: The revolutionary forces in the Philippines have ways to counteract the possibilities of foreign military intervention. First of all, the revolutionary forces and the people are self-reliant in waging the people's war. They know how to fight and defeat enemy forces that are superior to them militarily. Almost all the arms in the hands of the NPA have been taken from the enemy through tactical offensives.

Secondly, there must be an effective campaign to seek and gain solidarity from the peoples of the world, especially in the imperialist countries, in order to prevent or frustrate foreign military intervention or aggression. Remember how in recent history the Vietnamese people were able to defeat the US war of aggression through their self-reliant struggle and in active solidarity with the American people and other peoples of the world.

Thirdly, anti-imperialist governments that maintain an anti-imperialist stand and socialist aspirations may be willing to extend appropriate military assistance to the armed revolution in the Philippines. Such assistance does not run counter to self-reliance so long as the revolutionary forces are not dependent on it and make good use of it to expand and consolidate revolutionary strength.

Fourthly, the inter-imperialist contradictions may result in wars elsewhere to draw the attention of the imperialist powers away from the armed revolution in the Philippines.

8. Assuming that you reach the stage of strategic stalemate, how would you develop it and proceed to the strategic offensive?

JMS: I think that in the stage of the strategic stalemate regular mobile warfare will become prominent, at first with the use of companies and then with battalions. The larger formations for tactical offensives will result in the capture of more and better arms from the enemy side at a faster rate than in the guerrilla warfare at the stage of the strategic defensive. The stage of strategic stalemate will be far shorter than the stage of strategic defensive.

Entire enemy camps would be overrun, although not yet the biggest ones, and then armories taken over. To make NPA units ever available for tactical offensives, they will conduct a war of fluid movement. They will not occupy any area conspicuously long enough to attract enemy counter-attack and will continuously turn over control of an area to the people's democratic government, the people's militia, the revolutionary mass organizations and patriotic alliances. By that time, these revolutionary forces shall have become stronger and more capable of internal security and self-defense and attending to the needs of the people.

As soon as the NPA battalions become more prominent than NPA companies in tactical offensives, the NPA shall already be bringing the stage of the strategic stalemate to maturity and would be ready to enter the stage of the strategic offensive with battalions and regiments capable of wiping out the strategic enemy holdouts, which by that time would increasingly be purely on the defensive and become ripe for the taking.

But, of course, foreign military intervention should not be discounted. When that happens, the NPA has to adjust its strategy and tactics. The foreign aggressor troops would come in superior strength and bomb the strong points of the NPA. Anticipating these well in advance, the NPA forces would have to make themselves unavailable for easy targeting, operate as smaller but more widespread and more mobile fighting units to be able to deal lethal blows to the foreign enemy forces at every phase and stage in the national war of liberation against foreign aggression.

9. What are the political and military prerequisites for socialist revolution and construction upon the basic completion of the people's democratic revolution?

JMS: It must be clear that the people's democratic revolution is basically completed upon the overthrow of the ruling system of big compradors, landlords and corrupt bureaucrats. Thus, the people's democratic government, which is the incipient socialist government, would have the political authority and military power to secure the borders of the country, take over the commanding heights of the economy, control inflation, start the rehabilitation of the country, complete the revolutionary land reform program, ensure full employment, allow some small private enterprises and trading to revive the economy if necessary for a definite period, accommodate certain entrepreneurs in joint-state private companies, and start as soon as possible new and necessary industries.

It is important to undertake the aforesaid transitory measures in order to lay the ground for socialist revolution and construction. To undertake the socialist revolution, the working class and its advance detachment, the CPP, must consolidate political power on the basis of the worker-peasant alliance and avail of the mass movement, the educational system, the mass media, all forms of cultural and artistic work to raise the revolutionary consciousness of the people.

Taking over the commanding heights of the economy, including the financial system, the strategic enterprises, the sources of raw materials and the transport lines provide the CPP and the proletariat with the levers for undertaking socialist construction under centralized state planning. The main objective of socialist construction shall be to develop the heavy and basic industries stage by stage in a comprehensive way; and to carry out cooperativization and mechanization of agriculture consequent to the completion of land reform and national industrialization.

10. Will it still be possible for the people's democratic government to avail of economic and diplomatic relations with industrial capitalist countries?

JMS: It is absolutely necessary to proclaim and carry out as far as possible an independent foreign policy of maintaining economic and diplomatic relations with all countries and foreign governments, irrespective of ideology and political and social systems. That means having relations with industrial capitalist countries.

While certain imperialist countries might persist in their hostile policy and use embargo blockades or sanctions against the Philippine socialist state, there will also be other industrial capitalist countries willing to carry on economic and diplomatic relations in the pursuit of their national interest or to get economic relief from the worsening crisis of overproduction.

The Philippine socialist economy will certainly seek to export its products and acquire more efficient capital equipment and higher technology and even some consumer products that the domestic economy does not yet produce. There can be a fair exchange of goods and services to the mutual interest and mutual benefit of the Philippines and its economic partners.

Even hostile foreign powers can change and agree to maintain economic and diplomatic relations with the Philippine socialist state. Remember that the foreign interventionist powers that invaded the Soviet Union eventually changed their policies during the years of the Great Depression, Stalin was able to carry on normal economic and trade relations and even to acquire capital equipment from the industrial capitalist countries, without compromising the socialist character of the Soviet Union.

11. Can you give me an outline of what would be the foreign policy of the people's democratic government? What moral and material contributions are expected from foreign parties, organizations and individuals in solidarity with such a government?

JMS: The foreign policy of the prospective Philippine socialist republic will follow definite principles, such as independence and equality of all countries, and development of relations of cooperation, noninterference and mutual benefit among them, diplomacy and negotiations or litigation before international courts as the method for resolving differences, shunning wars of aggression and using the conditions of peace for general development of all economies, the elimination of poverty, and improvement of the living standards of all peoples.

To be able to realize and support the foreign policy both of the Philippine socialist republic and the CPP and its allied parties, organizations and individuals must promote international solidarity for peace and development with their foreign counterparts. The relations must be mutually interesting and satisfactory and conducive to world peace and cooperation among all countries. As a working-class party dedicated to the socialist cause, the CPP as the leading party will make it a point to promote and advance proletarian internationalism and mutual support and benefit with other socialist countries and all communist and workers parties and groups abroad.

12. What contributions will such a government expect from the overseas Filipinos? Many of them have knowledge and skills very suitable and useful for the economic, political and cultural well-being and development of the Philippines.

JMS: It is true that the overseas Filipinos possess knowledge and skills very much suitable, useful and urgently needed for the economic, political and cultural well-being and development of the Philippines. The Philippine socialist republic will call upon them, including their families and friends, to contribute what they can to the progress of their motherland. I am certain that in the first place most of them, if not all, would be eager to help their own motherland and share their knowledge and skills.

Filipino academics, experts and achievers in every field of natural and social sciences and humanities will come over to contribute their knowledge and skills. The scientists, technologists and health professionals among them can transfer their higher level of practice and technology to their motherland even before the socialist republic can work out agreements and arrangements with foreign corporations.

The many overseas Filipino workers who have taken on foreign jobs that are below their educational and training levels will gain the opportunity to apply whatever they had previously learned in the Philippines as well as abroad in recent times. They can forego continuing to suffer separation from relatives and friends in the Philippines and face uncertain conditions abroad.

★ ★ ★

Chapter IX

Prospects for a worldwide socialist resurgence

1. What is the current status of the US on the world stage, after being regarded as the sole superpower? Has it been successful in maintaining its global hegemony through the neoliberal economic policy and the neoconservative policy of aggressive wars? Is it currently slipping into a state of strategic decline in a multipolar world?

JMS: The US is still the No. 1 imperialist power economically and militarily in relation to every other imperialist power. But it has declined from its previous peak, especially in economic terms. It has ceased to be the sole superpower that can do anything unilaterally as in the years from 1991 to 2008 and face no counteraction from other imperialist powers. Now, it has to take into account the direct and indirect counteractions of other imperialist powers in a multipolar world as in Syria and Venezuela today. Within this context, the US will increasingly knock on the limits of its economic and military power but will not be able to stop its further strategic decline.

The US has never really solved its problem of stagflation since the latter half of the 1970s. This arose from the crisis of overproduction as a result of the post-war recovery and reconstruction of the industrial capacity of the imperialist countries (especially Germany and Japan) which were devastated in World War II. The use of monetarist and neoliberal policies have only served to cover up the problem with the use of finance capital or abuse of credit in the world capitalist system. The further rise in productive capacity of the traditional capitalist powers, especially the adoption of higher labor-saving technology, have resulted in more frequent and worse economic and financial crisis, including layoffs, retrenchment and ever graver job insecurity and unemployment.

The economic competition and political rivalry among the imperialist powers have intensified with the emergence of new imperialist powers, China and Russia. The US is now regretful that it had conceded consumer manufacturing to China in the bid to integrate it into the world capitalist system since the late 1970s and has also allowed China to enjoy large export surpluses and acquire new equipment and higher technology at a faster rate since the 1990s.

The US now has a very distorted economy, having weakened its manufacture of consumer and other tradeable goods, which used to employ the main part of American workers, and having magnified war production by the military-industrial complex, which employs less people than in the manufacture of tradeable civilian goods. Chronic unemployment, the dwindling of the middle class and increase of mass poverty have worsened. In pressing down employment and wage incomes and increasing the organic composition of capital, the US domestic market has tended to shrink. The US has suffered a widening trade deficit, incurred mainly in its economic and trade relations with China.

Within the context of the US economy, stepped up war production and state purchases of weapons have been lucrative to the military industrial complex but the wars of aggression unleashed by the US since the 1990s, have not resulted in profitable expansion of economic territory abroad. The expense of US$ 6.0 trillion for the wars of aggression since 9-11 have been counterproductive and have exacerbated the US budgetary deficits and public debt problems. In addition, China has used its export trade surpluses to buy public securities and bonds from the US and to invest in its own economy and in various countries of the world.

As in the time of the Cold War, the US has no monopoly of nuclear and other weapons of mass destruction. Russia has maintained and improved on these weapons and delivery systems. Thus, in Syria, the US has run into a solid wall of Russia-Syria alliance, which it can neither defeat with highly destructive conventional weapons nor discourage with threats to use weapons of mass destruction. China has also improved its weaponry with higher technology and is an effective Russian security partner in Eurasia and on a wider scale.

2. Did monopoly capitalism really kill the socialist cause and ideas once and for all with such tools as neocolonialism, neoliberalism, modern revisionism and even right-wing populism? Or does the entry of two more imperialist powers in the top circle give rise to a multipolar world and intensified contradictions among the imperialist circles?

JMS: The entry of China and Russia into the top circle of imperialist powers has made the world capitalist system more afflicted by the crisis of overproduction and abuse of finance capital. This has resulted in greater social disorder, political turmoil and continuous wars of aggression in the world capitalist system. For a while, the imperialist powers seemed to unite under the flag of neoliberalism against the world proletariat and oppressed peoples and nations but eventually the inter-imperialist contradictions have become conspicuous and intensified.

Monopoly capitalism has not killed the cause of anti-imperialism and socialism but has caused a serious setback to it by using a series of tools like neocolonialism, neoliberalism, modern revisionism, social democracy and even Right-wing populism. The most lethal of these tools has been modern revisionism because it worked like poison and destroyed from within the former bulwarks of socialism, which were the strongest in opposing imperialism. The destruction of socialism in these countries generated adverse effects on a wide scale, including on all the peoples fighting for national and social liberation.

But it is now clear that with the increase in the number of imperialist powers, economic crises, state terrorism and wars of aggression have become rampant, and the imperialist powers inflict even greater suffering on the proletariat and people and incite them to rise up in resistance and fight for national liberation, democracy and socialism against imperialism and all reaction.

3. China became the main partner of the US in promoting the line of neoliberal globalization for a long time in accordance with its policy of capitalist reforms and opening up to the capitalist world. In what way has China put one over the US to the extent that US President Donald Trump is now adopting protectionist measures to take back the previous US economic, trade and technological concessions to China?

JMS: US imperialism was overeager to win its Cold War with the Soviet Union and was willing to give accommodations to China and make it a stronger ally against the Soviet Union. Thus, the US readily welcomed the overthrow of the revolutionary proletariat in China in 1976 and China's capitalist reforms and integration into the world capitalist system. It conceded consumer manufacturing to China and together with its allies began to invest in the Chinese economy.

China put one over the US by maintaining a two-tier economy of state-owned enterprises (SOE) and private enterprises. It uses the SOEs to achieve strategic goals in economic and military production. Even under US pressure to privatize SOEs, China has maintained the dominant position of state monopoly capitalism. To this day, the

SOEs are supposed to be only three percent of all corporations but it continues to account for about 30 percent of industrial production.

Thus, the US under Trump has expressed the view that it has been cheated and has declared a protectionist policy and trade war against China in order to reduce its export advantages and to stop the transfer of higher technology to it. Trump has demanded that China let go of the preferential advantages of its SOEs so as to weaken their ability to contend with their US counterparts in technology and sales. Nonetheless, the US and China will continue to negotiate to prevent their economic and diplomatic relations from deteriorating even further.

In such negotiations, the US will push China towards privatizing the SOEs and allow US corporations greater access to the Chinese market or else China's access to the US market will be greatly reduced, its export surpluses will also drop and its surplus capital for reinvestment in its Belt and Road Initiative (BRI) and other projects will decline. But China has also its points of strength to counter US demands. The US cannot damage the Chinese economy or drain its dollar holdings too fast because the US would also be adversely affected. The two will try to maintain amicable relations but the fast-rising crisis and wars will tend to upset their balance of strength and weaken the existing agreements.

4. Do you agree with Prof. Graham T. Allison's view that the US is now in a Thucydides trap with China, causing suspicion between the two and driving each one to counter what the other is undertaking?

JMS: The US and China have already reached the stage where Prof. Allison's "Thucydides Trap" has begun to operate. They have emerged as the main rivals for global hegemony. The multipolar world is reverting to a bipolar world but this time of two imperialist powers. The US suspects and worries about China's initiatives in the SCO, BRICS and BRI. It worries most about the China-Russia alliance. China likewise suspects and worries about the US initiatives in the East Asia-Pacific region and in countries bordering China in Central Asia.

In keeping with its alliance with Russia, China is mindful of US and NATO threats to Russia on its own borders and in several global regions. While keeping its alliance with China, the US tends to team up with Japan against China on a number of issues. It is asserting the freedom of navigation to counter China's excessive claim that it owns 90 percent of the South China Sea and it is also seeking to undercut from year to year the surplus capital that China is deploying on a wide scale and to upset and derail the BRI initiative with offers of lower interest loans for infrastructure projects to client-states under the auspices of the World Bank and traditional imperialist powers.

China will continue to stay within the WTO to avail of provisions for control and manipulation of less developed countries in lopsided agreements. It will continue to keep within the AIIB and the New Development Bank the noncontrolling investments from other multilateral banks but will certainly secure and strengthen its controlling investments.

The US is wary of the high-tech weaponry that China has developed. It is trying to ensure its own superiority even as the alliance of China and Russia deters the US from attacking any of the two. With regard to military preparedness, the US and China maintain their own respective military forces and high-tech weaponry but each actually possess more than these through their alliances, such as the US with Japan and the European Union; and China with Russia.

5. The US has maintained an unfriendly attitude to Russia reminiscent of the Cold War. Why does the US use every possible way to pressure Russia on its borders? Why the extension of the NATO to the borders of Russia after the dissolution of the Warsaw Pact? Why the so-called color revolutions, the US intervention in Ukraine and the US-NATO military exercises on the borders of Russia?

JMS: It is not only due to force of habit from the Cold War that the US is undertaking many actions hostile and offensive to Russia, like the extension of NATO to the Russian borders, the color revolutions so-called, sanctions against Russian repossession of Crimea, the US intervention for the neofascists in Ukraine, the US economic sanctions on Russia and the frequent US-NATO military exercises on Russian borders.

In the inter-imperialist conflict of interests, US imperialism is now facing Russian imperialism shorn of socialist pretenses. US imperialism wishes to increase its investments and influence within Russia and the former Soviet Union. But as in China, the one thing that the Russian bourgeoisie has learned well from the previous socialist period is upholding and defending national sovereignty, especially on the basis of an industrial base, abundance of oil and gas, possession of nuclear and other weapons of mass destruction, and more efficient methods of delivery.

Russian imperialism takes its own initiatives, which US imperialism opposes. It partners with China bilaterally and multilaterally in such formations as the Shanghai Cooperation Organization (SCO) and BRICS. It is a key player in providing oil and gas to Europe via the so-called North and South Streams (pipelines). It stands with Syria and counters the US-Israel scheme of eliminating all vestiges of the former Soviet influence in the Middle East and Africa. It sides with the Venezuela Bolivarian government against US imperialism.

6. China and Russia are in close partnership with regard to BRICS, New Development Bank (formerly BRICS Development Bank), Shanghai Cooperation Organization, the Belt and Road Initiative and the Asian Infrastructure Investment Bank (AIIB). How will the partnership of China and Russia go against the traditional partnership of US, Japan and the European Union and the UN Security Council and multilateral agencies and military alliances that they control in the various global regions?

JMS: Indeed, close China-Russia partnership is pronounced in BRICS, the New Development Bank, the Belt and Road Initiative and the Asian Infrastructure and Investment Bank. This goes against the US-Japan-EU traditional partnership in the world capitalist system, in the G-7 and the OECD, in the UN Security Council, in such multilateral agencies as IMF, World Bank and WTO and in the military alliances in various regions.

The Eurasian cooperation of China and Russia and the BRI are practically seeking to change the center and main pattern of the global economy and trade from the maritime trade since the 16th century, augmented by air power since the 20th century, which the Western powers have dominated. The BRI is going to facilitate the expansion of Chinese economic imperialism and the direct trade of both China and Russia on land by rails, roads, bridges and seaports to the rest of the Asian mainland, Africa and Europe or to most of the world. This leaves the US stranded between the Pacific and Atlantic Oceans.

The US is vehemently against this development. Thus, it is becoming protectionist and trying to cut down China's export surplus from the US market, which is the main source of the surplus capital that enables China to undertake the BRI project. The US is also alarmed by the Made in China 2025 plan, which it is countering with its own Made in America plan to revive US manufacturing of tradeable goods.

7. How will the balance of power between the US and China operate in the contradictions over the South China Sea, Korean Peninsula and the Asia-Pacific region? Will the revolutionary forces in the region be affected?

JMS: The Asia-Pacific region has been the biggest place in carrying on the biggest part of the world economy and trade passing through the South China Sea lane. This region is inevitably a major site of cooperation and contention among the imperialist powers. Contention is becoming more conspicuous as the crisis of the world capitalist system worsens.

Backed by its so-called economic rise and increased military capability, China has been claiming ownership of 90 percent of the South China Sea and then depriving the Philippines and other Southeast Asian countries of their exclusive economic zones and extended continental shelves (ECSs) in accordance with the UN Convention on the Law of the Sea (UNCLOS). The Permanent Arbitration Court in The Hague has already ruled in favor of the Philippines against China and has invalidated China's "historical claims."

The US, Japan and the EU are united in asserting the right of free navigation in the South China Sea and support the rights of the Southeast Asian countries to their respective EEZs and ECS, especially the sovereign rights of the Philippines over the West Philippine Sea, which are in accordance with the UNCLOS and the arbitral tribunal ruling.

As far as the South China Sea is concerned, China has worked itself into a bad position by making claims far in excess of its own EEZ and ECS and by building and militarizing artificial islands in violation of the sovereign rights of the Philippines. In this regard, the Philippine revolutionary forces assert the principle of national sovereignty and demand that China respect this and they condemn the Duterte regime as a traitor for selling out sovereign rights. They explain to the Filipino people that China has long become capitalist and imperialist and that it is their patriotic duty to stand up and fight against such violation.

With regard to the Korean Peninsula, China is in a good position as it generally supports the Democratic People's Republic of Korea in the struggle against the aggressive policy and actions of the US imperialists. By its own principles and efforts, the DPRK has stood firmly and effectively against the US military blockade, nuclear threat, military provocations, economic embargo and various sanctions. It has outmaneuvered the US by availing of the support of China and Russia and promoting peaceful reunification of the two Koreas in cooperation with the current government in the South. The Philippine revolutionary forces support the DPRK and China in this regard.

While the Western powers and Japan are assertive of the right of free navigation in the South China Sea and respect the EEZs and ECS of the Southeast Asian countries under UNCLOS, the Philippine revolutionary forces consider them as an important shield against the excessive claims and aggressive actions of China. But, of course, they remain alert and opposed to the exploitative and aggressive character and actions of all imperialist powers, especially the US which retains overall and multifaceted dominance over the Philippines through economic, cultural and military treaties, agreements and arrangements bilaterally and through certain multilateral agreements.

8. The crisis and turbulence of the world capitalist system has become so serious that Francis Fukuyama has given up the notion that socialism is dead and capitalism is forever and has opened up to socialism as an alternative. Even Bill Gates believes that only socialism can solve the problem of global warming. Is there a trend of changing mood from pro-capitalism to pro-socialism in the world?

JMS: Definitely, such trend is obvious, especially among the toiling masses and the middle social strata in various countries. This is the result of the worsening crisis of the world capitalist system and the continuous US and NATO wars of aggression since the disintegration of the Soviet Union. Many people are now hoping and aiming for the socialist alternatives to capitalism and are seriously studying the works of Marx, Engels, Lenin, Stalin and Mao and the historical experience of socialist revolution and construction.

Socialism is desired and being validated by the escalating capitalist forms of exploitation and oppression, the continuing wars of aggression and the growing threats of nuclear war and global warming as a result of wanton capitalist plunder of the world's natural resources and the environment. Thus, even Francis Fukuyama now considers the socialist alternative, whereas Bill Gates has been so frustrated in his futile attempts to persuade his fellow big bourgeois to refrain from ruining the environment that he has declared socialism as the only way to counter global warming.

The only way to get rid of capitalism and imperialism and achieve national liberation, democracy and socialism is for the proletariat and the rest of the people to rise up and take power. This is the way to end class exploitation and oppression as well as the threats of nuclear or environmental catastrophe from the monopoly bourgeoisie and their political agents.

9. Lenin pointed out that imperialist crisis and wars lead to revolutionary wars. Are the working classes and oppressed peoples moving in that direction?

JMS: The working classes and oppressed peoples are already angry at the long-running escalation of their exploitation and oppression and desire revolutionary change. It is up to the revolutionary forces to exert their best efforts to arouse, organize and mobilize the discontented masses. Otherwise they will just be preoccupied with trying to survive in the absence of definite forces and efforts to show them the way to resist their exploiters and oppressors effectively.

Lenin's dictum that imperialist crises and wars lead to revolutionary wars remains valid. But the revolutionary party of the proletariat must set the correct general line and the strategy and tactics in order to win the battle for democracy and proceed to the socialist revolution. Such party must increase and expand its corps of cadres and members by developing the revolutionary mass movement and mobilizing them for the mass struggles. The leading party and the revolutionary masses will certainly grow from small and weak to big and strong through mass struggles until they can achieve national and social liberation.

10. What in your view are the most promising anti-imperialist and pro-socialist movements in Asia as well as in Latin America and Africa?

JMS: The most promising anti-imperialist and pro-socialist movements in Asia are those in the Philippines, India and other South Asian countries because they are already in the process of waging people's war to carry out the people's democratic revolution. In Southeast Asia, the Indonesians can easily catch up if it had a party like the CPP that is ready to start people's war in at least three regions. They should avoid any decisive engagement in one place like Blitar in 1968.

In the Middle East, the Kurdish and Turkish revolutionary parties and armed movements have suffered from the wars of national oppression and imperialist aggression. At the same time, they have taken advantage of the inter-imperialist contradictions and the armed conflicts in the Middle East in order to increase their own political and armed strengths.

In Latin America there are parties and movements engaged in revolutionary armed struggle in certain countries. Even in Colombia, where the FARC has been disintegrated by a peace agreement with the reactionary government, some armed movements are still continuing the armed struggle. In the meantime, the Bolivarian government in Venezuela is resisting the attempts of the US and the local reactionaries to topple it. It invokes the national sovereignty and socialist aspirations of the Venezuelan people.

In Africa, some parties are striving to strengthen themselves and to organize the armed revolutionary movement. They can take advantage of the widespread availability of firearms due to the proxy wars being generated by inter-imperialist contradictions. Under these conditions, they can build their own people's army, mass organizations and local organs of political power.

11. You mentioned Indonesia. Considering the fact that the Partai Komunis Indonesia (PKI) once was the third largest Communist party worldwide, what went wrong and finally enabled Suharto and his clique of co-generals to almost physically wipe out the PKI and install a brutal regime anchored on state-terrorism? Paradoxically, it seems that it was in Indonesia where – at the height of the US aggression against the peoples of Vietnam, Cambodia and Laos – the "Vietnam War" was won.

JMS: Frankly speaking, US imperialism more than made up for its prospective defeat in Vietnam in 1975 in advance by earlier destroying the Communist Party of Indonesia (PKI) in 1965, massacring three million cadres, members and mass sympathizers. Indonesia is a far bigger country, with more people and more natural resources than Vietnam. Thus, US imperialism was able to prevail over the cause of national liberation in the whole of Southeast Asia by carrying out the massacres against PKI.

The PKI was vulnerable to destruction because the leadership had a poor grasp of the revolutionary essence of Marxism-Leninism. It recruited its huge membership of millions mainly for electoral struggle and was almost totally exposed to the reactionaries from the village level to the national level, it had no people's army or any system of armed self-defense and subordinated itself to the Sukarno-led united front called Nasionalisme, Agama, dan Komunisme (NASAKOM – acronym for Nationalism, Religion, Communism). What I say comes mainly from the self-criticism of the PKI Political Bureau in 1966.

The PKI leadership was at a loss when the CIA-directed Suharto engineered the fake coup of Colonel Untung supposedly in defense of Sukarno against certain generals. Suharto followed this up with a real coup by using the strategic forces under his command. At the decisive moment, when the massacres were already being carried out against the PKI and its mass formations, the PKI Political Bureau decided in November 1965 to let Sukarno solve the problem of the Gestapu (the false flag coup) even as in fact Suharto had already usurped martial law powers and had disempowered him.

12. How do you look at the political trends in the imperialist countries? Will the people there rise up at a faster pace against the threat of nuclear war and global warming?

JMS: In the imperialist countries, the proletariat and the rest of the people are sick and tired of their own exploitation and deteriorating social conditions. But the monopoly bourgeoisie still has a lot of ideological, political and organizational weapons for distracting the people. At any rate, they try to mislead the people with a menu of parties that are conservative, social democratic, petty-bourgeois and populist or even outrightly fascist.

But a clear manifestation of the desperation of the monopoly bourgeoisie in the worsening crisis of the capitalist system and the potential rise of proletarian parties and revolutionary movements is the use of all means of education and information to promote personal greed, egotism, chauvinism, racism, anticommunism and fascism in both subtle and overt ways.

There is a marked rise in the political competition of the fascist and antifascist parties, organizations, and movements in the imperialist countries. Both the ideological and political influence of neoliberalism and its material consequences have generated the conditions for the rise of both the fascist and antifascist currents and movements. Under these conditions, the revolutionary party and its mass organizations can arise and grow in strength amidst the social discontent and political turmoil.

13. Do you think we are in a period of transition towards a resurgence of the forces of anti-imperialism, democracy and socialism? If so, what are the indications?

JMS: We are now in a period of transition towards a period of great resurgence of the revolutionary forces of anti-imperialism, democracy and socialism. The worsening crisis of capitalism under the neoliberal policy regime and the continuing imperialist wars of aggression have unprecedentedly wrought so much suffering among the people that the entire world has turned combustible in revolutionary terms and the people are driven to resist.

A time in the great resurgence will arise when the revolutionary movements in various countries will be racing each other in waging armed revolutions and aiming for victory. The peoples of the underdeveloped countries are still the most oppressed and exploited and can be expected to wage sustained revolutionary armed struggles more than those in the imperialist countries. But even in the imperialist countries, the social, economic and political conditions have so deteriorated at the unprecedentedly great expense of the people that revolution has become a desirable objective, especially in the weaker imperialist countries and in the former revisionist-ruled countries.

Right now, in the industrial capitalist countries, we are witnessing the growing contest between the forces of fascism and antifascism. Some demagogic fascist movements invoke the grievances of the people. Popular movements of a democratic kind also take up the grievances of the people and demand immediate reforms. The Occupy Movement arose previously and now the Yellow Vest Movement has risen. All these are indications of revolutionary potential and are the prelude to the rise of the revolutionary mass movement under the leadership of the revolutionary party of the proletariat.

★ ★ ★

Chapter X

Cultural issues and personal prospects

1. At your age of 80, have you started to reflect on what and how much you can still do? For decades you have not been involved in operational decisions of the revolutionary forces in the Philippines and you have decided to step down as Chairperson of the International League of Peoples' Struggle. But I guess you will certainly continue expressing your views on Philippine and global issues.

JMS: I feel that I have reached a new and higher level of intellectual maturity and articulateness. As a public intellectual committed to the struggle for national democracy and socialism, I will continue to analyze the Philippine and world situation and express my views accordingly.

I intend to continue accepting invitations to speak and write on issues and attend important occasions in the next five to ten years. I shall keep myself open to such invitations from Philippine and foreign organizations and publications and from the International League of Peoples' Struggles, its member-organizations and friends.

Appropriate to the situation, I shall speak and write as Founding Chairman of the Communist Party of the Philippines and Chief Political Consultant of the National Democratic Front of the Philippines (NDFP), as ILPS Chairperson Emeritus or as simply myself as a public intellectual with something significant or useful to express on Philippine and global issues.

2. What else do you intend to do? Aside from speeches and interviews, will you engage further in literary activities, creative writing, especially in poetry and essay writing ?

JMS: Because I will have no more executive functions in the ILPS and there will be no need for me to issue a statement on every major issue in the world, I shall gain the time to write poetry and probably even go back to my high school interest in painting.

Were it not for the travel restrictions due to absurd decisions on my asylum case, I would be travelling frequently and widely. But I can use the time saved from travelling for writing prose and poetry. Of course, I will continue to sing for fun at home alone or in the company of friends elsewhere.

My most serious plan is to oversee the selection and book publication of my speeches, articles, messages and statements and interviews under thematic titles from the periodic collections of my writings. That will be one definite way of further consolidating my written legacy. The themes will include Marxism-Leninism-Maoism, scientific socialism, the people's democratic revolution, the mass movement, people's war, culture and art and so on.

I will continue to give master classes to Filipino and non-Filipino activists and give interviews to postgraduate students for their dissertations as well as to curious journalists. Time will tell how I shall be active from year to year. In due time I shall fade away.

3. When back in 1987/88 we were in the process of writing the book The Philippine Revolution the Leader's View, I vividly remember that in your youth you'd wanted to join the priesthood and become a bishop. Your gifted and multi-talented co-Ilocano Isabelo de los Reyes combined both – secular and holy affairs – and was instrumental in building up important trade unions as well the IFI, the only church worldwide being the product of a prolonged anti-colonial and anti-imperialist struggle! Don't you envy him?

JMS: At the age of nine, I became a *sacristan* and memorized the Latin responses to the priest, though without understanding them. At any rate, I was religious enough under the influence of my mother. Then I was told later that my archbishop uncle, Juan Sison, of the archdiocese of Nueva Segovia, wished me to become a priest. I agreed and even harbored the illusion of becoming a bishop someday. But I changed my mind later when I realized that I also wanted to get married someday and would have difficulty following the vow of chastity as a priest.

Somehow at the age of ten, I was under the influence of the memory of Isabelo de los Reyes to a certain extent. He is my grand uncle because of the interrelations of my great grandfather Julian Sison with the Florentinos, Don Mena Crisologo and Don Isabelo de los Reyes of Vigan. My father told me how brilliant Don Belong was and how he became a *libre pensador* and sympathizer of the Philippine revolution and later, a senator. His stories were related to his close friendship with Isabelo, Jr. when they were still students in Manila.

When I was in the University of the Philippines from 1958 onwards, I learned from UP publications and from my professor-friends Teodoro Agoncillo and Leopoldo Yabes more about Isabelo de los Reyes. I found out that he was the founder of the modern trade union movement in the Philippines as well as the first to bring some works of Marx to the Philippines from Spain. I would come to know, too, that he was the founder of the Iglesia Filipino Independiente by writing the founding documents of this patriotic church, a fruit of the Philippine revolution that fought and won against Spanish colonialism and then resisted US imperialism. Thereafter, I grew even prouder of Isabelo de los Reyes than before.

In my undergraduate Spanish class, we translated to English as an exercise De los Reyes' memorial against friar rule and the friar estates. For writing this memorial soon after the outbreak of the Philippine revolution, he was arrested, detained and shipped to Barcelona for imprisonment in the Montjuich castle that served as prison house. He was released from prison after the outbreak of the Spanish-American War and was allowed to deliver speeches against US imperialism in Spain and France before returning to the Philippines.

4. In November 1987 the US-American author and journalist James Fallows published a controversial article in the Atlantic Monthly entitled "The Philippines–a damaged culture." Reading it again, one gets the impression that in large parts of his article Fallows is far from wrong. Considering that the incumbent president is fond of bullying his adversaries and whose language variety is rather restricted, how do you interpret the abovementioned article in the context of Mr. Duterte's public speeches and the impact they'll have as regards highly esteemed norms and traits like kapwa, hiya, utang na loob, damayan, especially among the youth?

JMS: James Fallows' "The Philippines—a damaged culture" is correct in describing and criticizing the dominant culture of the Philippines as having been molded by more than three centuries of Spanish colonialism and feudalism, by decades of direct US colonial rule and semifeudalism and finally, by the continuing oppressive and exploitative semicolonial and semifeudal ruling system of big compradors, landlords and corrupt bureaucrats who preserve the interests of US imperialism, domestic feudalism and bureaucrat capitalism.

Such a ruling system cannot but promote antinational and antidemocratic cultural values, attitudes and traits from the top level down to the lower levels of society, including the victimized masses of workers and peasants. These are fostered and reinforced through the government policies, and in the discourses and interactions in workplaces, marketplaces, schools, churches, the mass media and the electoral and other processes of the ruling system.

Indeed, servility to foreign interests, corruption and cronyism are transmitted downward to the broad masses of the people. These contaminate and distort the thinking, sentiments and behavior even of the victims of exploitation, oppression and impoverishment. Nonetheless, the broad masses of the people keep their moral and cultural bearing by looking after the non-exploitative interests of their own families for good or bad in relation to the national interest and the public good.

Duterte is so far the coarsest, most vulgar and most violent representative of the rotting ruling system, in terms of his foul language, his direct orders to his armed subordinates to perpetrate mass murder with impunity and his public assurance of presidential protection for their criminal actions. He has surpassed Marcos in many ways in brutality, especially to the poor people who are either listed as drug addicts and pushers or rebel suspects in order to show off his iron fist. But he is a cringing coward and a shameless traitor in relation to his imperialist masters and the plunderers who have made him president with money and bailiwick votes.

He acts both as a populist demagogue and as a clown when he speaks to his audiences. He resorts to vulgar and violent terms to attack his opponents and to dish out his lies as well as to make people laugh and entertained in a shallow way. He knows how to play on and manipulate the biases transmitted from the top to the bottom of the exploitative society and on the low level of information and education and narrow-mindedness that afflict the politically backward section of the toiling masses.

However, Fallows is one-sided by presenting only the negative side of Philippine culture. He only sees the dominant culture of the exploiting classes. He does not take into full account how the most exploited and most oppressed people rise up in so many uprisings that have peaked in the Philippine Revolution of 1896 and in the current people's democratic revolution.

He does not present and give due consideration to the great number of people in the armed revolutionary movement and the legal national democratic movement fighting for the national interest and the public good. They are guided by the demand for a national, scientific and pro-people culture and education in the program of the people's democratic revolution. They are imbued with a high level of morality and social enlightenment, including selflessness, resolve to serve the national community and humanity, and revolutionary courage and creativity.

5. One of the Philippines' most renowned writers and Magsaysay awardee, Francisco Sionil José, during several interviews with this author critically remarked about the elites and the left in his country – at least as the 1970s and the 1980s were concerned –, that the former were "too pro-US" and the latter "too pro-Chinese." Lately, Mr. José was harshly blamed in the media for comments to carry racist slurs or being outrightly "anti-Chinese." What is your view on these issues? Could you ever anticipate anti-Chinese pogroms in the Philippines similar to those which took place in neighbouring Indonesia during the Suharto dictatorship?

JMS: Francisco Sionil José is a long time notorious anti-communist and promoter of the CIA-organized Congress for Cultural Freedom. He has made a living from anticommunism. His bookstore on high rent Padre Faura Street has been practically subsidized by US foundations. He poses as someone critical of US imperialism. But in fact, he is not. He pretends to criticize the ruling elite as overly pro-US. But this false stance is merely meant to serve as a feint for attacking in an emotionally racist way the revolutionary movement as overly pro-Chinese.

Sionil José has always capitalized on his credentials as an anti-communist. He has been a rabid fan of Ramon Magsaysay (a political dummy of Colonel Edward Lansdale of the CIA) for supposedly crushing the armed revolutionary movement in the early 1950s with the use of brute force and deception through token land resettlement, misrepresented as land reform and designed to confuse landless peasants. In fact, it was the grave ideological, political and organizational errors of the Lava dynasticists in the old merger party of the communist and socialist parties that ultimately defeated the revolutionary movement in the early 1950s.

Sionil José fancies himself an adversary of landlordism. But in fact, he adopts the social-climbing sense and sensibilities of the rich peasant, the kulak or what Marx ridiculed as the relic of barbarism in 19th century French society. Sionil José's rich peasant mentality keeps him from understanding the fact that genuine land reform is impossible so long as the semicolonial and semifeudal ruling system persists.

He has no understanding of Mao both as a Chinese patriot and revolutionary, and as a proletarian internationalist. He does not comprehend even a little of Marxism-Leninism-Maoism. In publications he edited in the 1960s, he spread the sham propaganda that Mao wanted a nuclear war because there would still be hundreds of millions of Chinese left to rule the world.

In his anti-Chinese racism, he blinds himself to the obvious fact that Filipinos of Chinese ancestry start their patriotism with their love for and loyalty to their own Filipino mothers and only subsequently do they sympathize with their Chinese fathers or ancestors who had to leave China because of the hardships experienced there before the victory of the CPC-led Chinese revolution.

Many of those criticizing Duterte for his traitorous servility to now imperialist China in the mass media and social media are people of Chinese ancestry. They are the ones exposing how Duterte is selling out the sovereign rights of the Filipino people and making the Philippines a Chinese province and debt colony.

There can be no anti-Chinese racist pogroms in the Philippines as in colonial times when the Spanish colonizers deliberately turned the natives against the Chinese settlements in order to scapegoat them and distract attention from themselves as colonizers. It is more likely that the Chinese big bourgeoisie in China and in the Philippines would keep on acting in concert to bribe and manipulate the corrupt bureaucrats in the Philippines.

The Filipino people can very well differentiate the broad masses of the Chinese people and the Filipino people of Chinese ancestry from the Chinese policymakers and ruling-class responsible for Chinese monopoly capitalism or imperialism.

Anthropologists have claimed that Filipinos carry in them large doses of Chinese blood. Even Duterte is proud to be a recent descendant of a Chinaman called Lam and perhaps Sionil José, too has some Chinese blood running in his veins, very much like some Nazis in Hitlerite Germany who were later found to have Jewish blood upon close scrutiny of their genealogies.

6. Given the fact that the Philippines is a strongly family-centered society, how come you never mentioned or talked about your family?

JMS: I talk about my family whenever I am asked to. I share stories about the successes of my siblings in their respective professions and in other respects. I love to compare my economic poverty with the well-deserved professional and material success of my brother Dr. Ramon C. Sison who lived in Beverly Hills because he was a successful medical pathologist and hospital administrator and acted in some Hollywood films.

I am proud of the strong patriotic tradition in the Serrano-Sison family to which I belong, its record of siding with the people against Spanish colonialism, US imperialism and the Japanese fascist occupation. I am also proud of relatives who have honestly and competently served as mayors, congressmen, senators and cabinet members and who have excelled in various professions, especially medicine and law. But I am not proud of the feudal record of my direct Serrano-Sison family.

I can trace the family tree on the paternal and maternal sides of my father as well as my mother's from several generations back to the present, thanks to my late brother Ramon. He traced mainly the genealogies of the parents of my father in a short book, *Cabugao*, much less my mother's parents. He focused on the histories of the Serrano and Sison families. From Spanish colonial times, they were the principal families in the town where we were born and where we grew up.

In our family, the acknowledged patriarch was my great grandfather Don Leandro Serrano for the simple reason that he was the biggest landlord of the Ilocos region since the last quarter of the 19th century. He owned 80 percent of the agricultural land of Cabugao and sizeable parts of nearby towns like Lapog and Sinait, Ilocos Sur and Badoc, Ilocos Norte.

He held under tax declaration most of the shoreline from Badoc, Ilocos Norte to Sta Lucia, Ilocos Sur, a distance of some 80 to 100 kilometers. Here, he planted maguey and produced the fiber to make ropes that became stronger when steeped in sea water for which it was much in demand in the shipping industry until the cheaper abaca ropes from other regions became more available.

Don Leandro was the son of a Spanish-Mexican mestizo father who had come to the Philippines when the Manila-Acapulco trade dwindled in the first quarter of the 19th century. He married Ursula Azcueta, a descendant of a Spanish *sarhento mayor* of the Legazpi expedition, whose son started his family in Cabugao. This became the principal family in the town in the 17th century and onward. From generation to generation the Azcueta bloodline became mixed with those of Malay *indios*.

My great grandfather, Julian Sison, came to Cabugao from Vigan, Ilocos Sur circa 1870. He descended from a Chinese mestizo (Sangley) merchant from Lingayen, Pangasinan. The Sisons of Pangasinan were of Chinese origin. They could trace their lineage to a ship captain in the fleet of Lin Tao Kien in the 16th century.

In the course of his research, my brother was able to trace nine generations of Sisons from the Lingayen church records back to the 18th century. Don Julian married into the Soller family, which was then the wealthiest and principal family of Cabugao until the third quarter of the 19th century. The offspring of the Soller and Sison couple was my grandfather Don Gorgonio Serrano.

My grandfather was born in 1873, the first Sison to be born in Cabugao. He became the last gobernadorcillo under the Spanish colonial regime, the municipal president of the revolutionary government in 1899, and the first mayor under the US colonial regime in the early 20th century. My family is proudly feudalist, with all the divine Christian justification and with claims to be hard-working and astute above others. But I am not proud of that.

What I am proud of is that the Serrano and Sison families carry a strong patriotic tradition. They supported the Philippine revolution with food supplies and funds against Spanish colonialism, then against US imperialism and the guerrilla movement against the Japanese occupation.

My Serrano great grandfather and all his male children were arrested by the US imperialists and carried to the Marianas islands and my Sison grandfather was left to deal with the circumstances as they developed in the years from 1900 onwards. I grew up listening to stories how certain family members suffered torture and imprisonment or death in the hands of the foreign enemy.

7. What in your life annoyed you most and what is it that you cherished and liked best?

JMS: I have been annoyed and outraged by foreign domination of the Philippine ruling system and by the willingness of the reactionary government officials to be puppets and traitors to the Filipino people's interests; and finally by the ever-escalating class oppression and exploitation of the Filipino workers and peasants by the big compradors, landlords and the bureaucrat capitalists.

I cherish and like most the revolutionary tradition of the Filipino people and their persistence in the struggle for national and social liberation against all odds. The workers and peasants are most admirable for their willingness to struggle against their oppressors and exploiters and for taking the risks and making sacrifices, despite being so hard pressed to earn their day-to-day subsistence.

At the level of personal behavior, I am annoyed most by selfishness in various forms like arrogance and bullying, parasitism and money grubbing, unwillingness to help others in need, credit grabbing, intolerance, dogmatism and commandism, docility and obsequiousness, opportunism, laxity and negligence, lying to escape responsibility, reneging on promises and the like.

I cherish and like most the spirit of service and assistance not only to the people in general or in the abstract but also to those particular persons in need, extending kindness to them and exercising patience with them, doing their assignment well to help the team succeed, being considerate to others and promptness. I admire most the men and women who engage in revolutionary struggle, are ready to take the risks and make sacrifices and contribute their best they can to the advance of the revolution.

8. Knowing fully well, that Pinoys – the common Tao as well as Kasamas (Comrades) in the political underground – cherish jokes a lot and having developed a good sense of humor, which, by the way, is your favorite joke you would like to share here with our readers?

JMS: The question is unfair. I believe that I have such a healthy and bountiful sense of humor that I should not be limited to a single favorite among the thousands of jokes that I dish out during study and work sessions, moments of tension and periods of relaxation in my years in the underground and up to the present.

But here's one. In mock praise, we used to call Marcos the best recruiter of the New People's Army. Because everytime he launched a campaign of military suppression, there was a sharp increase of people joining the ranks of NPA. We also called him the best transport and supply officer of the NPA. Because by sending his troops to the guerrilla fronts, they came on their own transport and their weapons and other supplies for the NPA to capture.

Whenever the enemy troops advanced in superior force, they had the illusion of driving away the NPA and gaining ground because the NPA retreated. Then they camped and lost sleep every night because the NPA kept them awake with harassment fire. Then after being exhausted, they would leave and retreat. Finally, it was the turn of the NPA to have the last laugh by pursuing them, hitting them hard and capturing their arms.

9. How true is Duterte's claim that you have colon cancer? What exactly is your state of health?

JMS: Duterte invented his own story that I have colon cancer. When I had a phone conversation with him in December 2016, I only told him that I have been going to the hospital to have my treatment for inflammations and loss of appetite and weight due to rheumatoid arthritis. This is now under control.

I am healthy, with no life-threatening condition like cancer, blood disorder or cardiac problem. I only have to watch out for rheumatoid arthritis and the danger of pneumonia. My eyesight and hearing are functioning well with the aid of my eye glasses and hearing aid.

By his own public account, Duterte is the one with a colon problem. His colon is supposed to be blocked and the waste from his food intake goes back to his esophagus. This causes prolonged periods of constipation as well as cancer. As a matter of public interest, you should ask him or his doctor what is ailing him because he suffers from incoherent and self-contradictory speech, has facial discoloration and is wobbly when he walks.

10. Do you expect to live long enough to see a resurgence of the revolutionary movements of anti-imperialism, democracy and socialism and eventually the victory of the people's democratic revolution in the Philippines – at least a patriotic government that is progressive enough to allow your homecoming on friendly terms?

JMS: I hope to live long enough to see the great resurgence of the revolutionary movements on a global scale and see in the horizon the oncoming total victory of the people's democratic revolution in possibly ten to twenty years from now. Along the way to victory, it is also possible for a truly patriotic and progressive government to arise, after serious peace negotiations take place and an alliance for national unity, peace and development sincerely invites me to return home.

Conditions are such that Duterte was able to pretend as being patriotic and progressive in order to win the 2016 elections. After more than 50 years of arousing, organizing and mobilizing the people along the national democratic line, the CPP and other revolutionary forces have generated conditions that can allow parties and leaders that are truly patriotic and progressive to gain popular support and power for the public good.

11. Bourgeois politicians the world over measure their success by how much power and wealth they can gain for themselves, their clique and special class interests that back them up. How do you measure success in your personal lifelong struggle as a revolutionary?

JMS: I have never been interested in gaining personal wealth and power since childhood, although up to the age of 18 I aspired to become president to serve the people and make fundamental changes in society. Since the age of 19, I have measured success in terms of my revolutionary work being able to achieve what is possible under the conditions of chronic crisis in the Philippines and the external factors which are beyond the control of the Philippine revolutionary movement.

Together with comrades, I believe that we have achieved great success in creating and developing revolutionary forces, which are nationwide and are deeply rooted among the toiling masses of workers and peasants. Comrades in the Philippines have successfully continued the work that others and I started in building the revolutionary forces, such as the CPP, the NPA, the NDFP, the revolutionary mass organizations and the local organs of political power, which constitute the people's democratic government.

While compelled to be in exile, I have done my best in working to analyze, write and put forward proposals on the positions and courses of action concerning Philippine and global issues. I have participated in important conferences and seminars for the building of genuine revolutionary parties of the proletariat, combating imperialism, modern revisionism and reaction. I feel that I have contributed much as chairperson of the International League of Peoples' Struggle to developing and advancing the international anti-imperialist and democratic mass movement for national and social liberation.

12. What is your most important literary legacy? Are you still craving to make significant achievements in whichever field?

JMS: My literary legacy include my Marxist-Leninist-Maoist essays on theory, politics, economy and culture and, of course, my poetry. The most comprehensive collection of my poems until 2013 was published in The Netherlands by an adjunct publisher of the New World Academy in 2013. But since then, I have written new poems and intend to come out with a new volume in due time.

I am gratified that my essays and poems have been recognized for their social significance and literary qualities by the Manila Critics Circle in 1984, Writers Union of the Philippines in 1985 and The Southeast Asia WRITE Award in 1986. I also received other awards of recognition like the Marcelo H. del Pilar for my writings and the Guro ng Bayan (People's Teacher) Award from the Congress of Teachers and Educators for Nationalism (CONTEND). There are also awards for my work among the workers, peasants and youth from Kilusang Mayo Uno (KMU – May First Movement), Kilusang Magbubukid ng Pilipinas (KMP – Philippine Peasant Movement) and Kabataang Makabayan.

I am interested in singing and painting. But I do not think that I have achieved anything that is outstanding and worth preserving as serious legacy in these fields. Neither do I think that I will excel in these fields beyond entertaining a few comrades and friends in cozy sessions and as forms of relaxation.

13. What do you consider your most important legacy to the Filipino people? How can such legacy be preserved and developed? As far as you know, what are the concrete measures being undertaken to promote that legacy?

JMS: My most important legacy to the Filipino people is in the form of theoretical and political writings needed for the reestablishment and development of the CPP as a revolutionary party of the proletariat and for the creation and growth of all other necessary revolutionary forces, including the NPA, the NDFP, the mass organizations and the people's democratic government from the village level upward.

The best way to preserve and develop my legacy is to carry forward the people's democratic revolution and reach the stage of socialist revolution and construction. Of course, it is also important that the collection of my writings continues to be done and thematic selections are being made to serve as enhanced educational tools.

In its Second Congress, the CPP produced and issued a long resolution in appreciation of my theoretical and practical contributions to the advance of the people's democratic revolution with a socialist perspective. I am deeply grateful for such a resolution. You can a get a copy of this from www.philippinerevolution.net.[8]

☆ ☆ ☆

8 Included here, see pp. 159-167.-Editor

Appendices

About Rainer Werning

Dr. Rainer Werning was born in December 1949 in the West German city of Münster, which – along with the nearby city of Osnabrück – was the site of the signing of the Peace of Westphalia that ended the Thirty Years' War in 1648. He grew up in the Münsterland, whose charming plains border The Netherlands.

After being expelled from High School (Gymnasium) for political reasons, he embarked on several world trips, after which he worked in publishing houses as an editorial consultant, writer, author and lecturer.

A witness to the First Quarter Storm student protests against the Marcos regime and the "Diliman Commune" in the Philippines in the early 1970s, he became an active member of the international Philippines Solidarity Network, translated José Maria Sison's *Philippine Society and Revolution* into German (May 1973) and co-authored the book *The Philippine Revolution – The Leader's View* with José Maria Sison (1989).

In the late 1970s he pursued university studies, reading social and political science, literature and philosophy at the Universities of Münster and Osnabrück (where he obtained his Ph.D. in political science in 1984) and undertaking research, inter alia, at the Universities of Hull, Sophia (Tokyo) and Columbia (New York). In the early 1980s he enrolled at the University of the Philippines' Asian Center in Diliman, Quezon City.

He lectured at the Universities of Bonn and Osnabrück between 2010 and 2015, and is currently a lecturer on Philippine and (North-) Korean affairs at the Academy for International Cooperation (AIZ) in Bonn-Röttgen, Germany.

Werning is a specialist on Southeast and East Asian Affairs and has written several books on the two Koreas, Japan, Cambodia, Myanmar (formerly Burma), Indonesia and the Philippines. He is the co-editor of *Handbuch Philippinen*, the 6th edition of which appeared in February 2019.

★ ★ ★

Resume of José Maria Sison

General Description: Prof. José Maria Sison is a Filipino patriot, a proletarian revolutionary and internationalist. He is a Filipino statesman, known for his experience in and knowledge of the people's democratic government and revolutionary forces in the Philippines. He is sometimes consulted by high officials of foreign governments and by presidents, senators, congressmen and local officials of the Philippine reactionary government concerning peace negotiations with the National Democratic Front of the Philippines (NDFP) and related matters. He is recognized as the foremost thinker and leader of the Filipino people's movement for national liberation and democracy in the last 50 years.

After the destruction of the armed revolutionary movement in the early 1950s in the Philippines, he was chiefly responsible for the resurgence of the anti-imperialist and anti-feudal mass movement in the Philippines since 1959. He was the founding Chairman of the Central Committee of the CPP, 1968-77. He is one of the world's leading authorities on the theory and practice of Marxism-Leninism and Maoism, on revolutionary movements in Asia and on the international communist movement. He has been a recognized poet since 1962 and awardee of the Southeast Asia WRITE Award for poetry, 1986.

Current Positions and Activities: Prof. Sison is the Chairperson of the International Coordinating Committee, International League of Peoples' Struggle (ILPS), 2004 to the present. He is Chief Political Consultant, NDFP Peace Panel Negotiating with the Government of the Republic of the Philippines (GRP), 1995 to the present; and Chairman, Center for Social Studies, 1992 to the present. He is often asked to write and speak on current burning social issues in the Philippines and to deliver messages of solidarity to major Philippine institutions and organizations. Thus, he is in close touch with his people, despite the great geographic distance of his place of exile. As ILPS Chairperson, he expresses on a timely basis the position of the ILPS on major global issues. He is also often invited to speak on Philippine and global issues to academic and nonacademic audiences abroad.

Birth and Educational Achievement: Born of a landed but patriotic family in Cabugao, Ilocos Sur, Philippines, on February 8, 1939. He finished with honors the degree of Bachelor of Arts in English Literature in the University of the Philippines in 1959 and became a member of Phi Kappa Phi international honor society and the PI Gamma Mu international social science fraternity. He took masteral studies in comparative literature in 1959-61. He taught English grammar and literature in the University of the Philippines in 1959-61. He became press relations officer of the Araneta University in 1962-63 and professorial lecturer in political science in the Lyceum of the Philippines, 1964-67. He became an associate professor in political science in the Asian Center of the University of the Philippines in 1986-87. He was research consultant on development and socialization in the University of Utrecht, 1987-89. He was chairman of the International Network for Philippine Studies, from 1989 to 2014.

Leader of Mass Movement in the 1960s: Fearless of the Cold War and the Anti-Subversion Law of 1957 which penalized with death political dissent and revolutionary activity, Prof. Sison initiated Marxist study circles and the formation of mass organizations of youth, workers and peasants in order to revive the national democratic movement against US imperialism, feudalism and bureaucrat capitalism in the Philippines in the 1960s. He started as a student political activist in the University of the Philippines, where he formed study circles in Marxism and the Philippine revolution from 1958 onwards. He was the founding chairman of the Student Cultural Association of the University of the Philippines, 1959-62. He used this as a base for forming similar organizations in other universities and promoting student mass protests.

He joined the old merger party of the Communist and Socialist parties and became a member of its Central Executive Committee, 1962-67. He edited the Progressive Review, a Marxist journal of ideas and opinions on Philippine society, economy, politics, culture and foreign policy, from 1963 to 1968. He was in charge of research and education in the legal Workers' Party (Lapiang Manggagawa) and carried out study courses among the leaders and activists of the trade union, peasant and youth movements from 1962 onwards. He was founding chairman of Kabataang Makabayan (Patriotic Youth) in 1964. He became general secretary and then vice chairman of Socialist Party of the Philippines (formerly Worker's Party) in 1965. He promoted the national united front and became general secretary of the anti-imperialist united front, Movement for the Advancement of Nationalism in 1966-68.

Leader of the Revolutionary Movement: Prof. Sison led the First Great Rectification Movement among the Filipino communists from 1966 to 1968 in order to criticize, repudiate and rectify the major ideological, political and organizational errors and weaknesses of the leadership of the old communist party from 1930 onwards and thereby lay the basis for the reestablishment of the communist party under the guidance of Marxism-Leninism-Mao Zedong Thought. He advocated the general line of new democratic revolution under working class leadership through protracted people's war and with socialist perspective. He became the founding Chairman of the Central Committee of the Communist Party of the Philippines, which was reestablished on December 26, 1968.

He was chairman of the CPP Military Commission that founded the New People's Army on March 29, 1969. In representation of the CPP, he co-founded the National Democratic Front of the Philippines on April 24, 1973 as an underground united front organization against the Marcos fascist dictatorship. He was responsible for the mobile office of the central leadership and marched with the revolutionary cadres, Red fighters and masses in various regions of the Philippines. He shared the fighting tasks, the difficulties, the risks and the victories of the armed revolution during its foundational period. He was captured by the Marcos fascist dictatorship on November 10, 1977, subjected to various forms of torture (including punching, water cure, in shackles and fetters for more nearly two years and solitary confinement for than five years) and detained until the fall of Marcos in February 1986.

Activities After Release from Detention: Engaged in public speeches, academic lectures, press interviews and writing articles on the Philippine situation, its problems, possible solutions and prospects. Reinstated as faculty member with the rank of associate professor in political science in the Asian Center of the University of the Philippines in 1986. Chairman of the Preparatory Committee that founded the Partido ng Bayan (People's Party). He declined to be chairman of the party and started his lecture tour on the Philippines in Asia-Pacific, India and Europe which lasted from 1986 to 1988. He became research consultant on socialization and development in the University of Utrecht from 1987 to 1989. He continues to give occasional lectures on various topics in Dutch and other European universities.

Continuing Oppression Abroad: Philippine authorities were angered by the lectures of Prof. Sison, cancelled his passport and subjected him to the false charge of subversion and threats of arbitrary arrest and torture. He applied for political asylum in The Netherlands in 1988. He became recognized as a political refugee by the highest Dutch administrative court in 1992 and again in 1995. But the Dutch government has refused to grant him asylum and residence. The US, Philippine and Dutch Philippine governments have levelled false charges against him in order to oppress him and discourage him from exercising his civil rights. As a result of lobbying by the US and Philippine governments, he was listed as a terrorist by the Dutch government and then by the Council of European Union in 2002.

The European Court of First Instance ruled on July 11, 2007 that he was illegally listed as terrorist and subjected to sanctions because his rights to be informed of the charge, to legal defense and to availment of judicial protection were violated. Then upon the request of the Philippine government, the Dutch authorities arrested him on August 28, 2007 and detained him for two weeks on a false charge of ordering the killing of military agents or security contractors of the Philippine government. The Philippine Supreme Court had ordered on June 2, 2007 the dismissal of the charge of rebellion, which incorporated the aforesaid charge recycled by the Dutch authorities. He was released on September 13, 2007 due to lack of evidence and due to worldwide public outrage over the false charge. The US and Philippine governments continue to oppress him with threats of prosecution and imprisonment with the use of false charges in a brazen bid to pressure the NDFP to capitulate to the Philippine government.

The false charge of ordering the killing of military agents in the Philippines against Prof. Sison was dropped by the Dutch Prosecution Service on March 30, 2009 in line with previous decisions of the Dutch examining judge, The Hague District Court and the Court of Appeal. The European Court of Justice ruled on September 30, 2009 that the name of Prof. Sison be removed from the terrorist blacklist of the European Union because he was never investigated, prosecuted or convicted for any act of terrorism and because Dutch court decisions that have nothing to do with terrorism cannot be used against him.

Outstanding Activities Abroad: Prof. Sison has been the chairperson of the International Network for Philippine Studies since 1989 and the Center for Social Studies since 1992. He has been a successful individual plaintiff in the human rights case against the Marcos estate in the US court system. He provided the crucial testimony on his torture that proved the direct responsibility of Marcos for human rights violations. He has authored several books and articles published in various languages by US, European and Asian publishers. He has been a participant in major poetry festivals. He has contributed papers to conferences and seminars. He has discussed various theoretical issues concerning socialism and capitalism and strategic issues involving the people's struggle for national and social liberation against imperialism and reaction, particularly against the US-instigated imperialist globalization and global war of terror.

He was chairman of the International Conference of Marxist-Leninist Parties and Organizations from 1992 to 1994 and Chairman of the International Seminar on Mao Zedong Thought in 1993. He was a consultant of the Brussels Communist Seminar from 1994 to 2002. He was chairperson of the International Initiative Committee that founded the ILPS in 2001 and became General Consultant of ILPS from 2001 to 2004. He was elected Chairperson of ILPS by its Second International Assembly in Eindhoven in 2004 and reelected to the same position by the Third International Assembly in Hong Kong 2008. ILPS has become veritably the biggest international united front of people's organizations along the anti-imperialist and democratic line.

Role in GRP-NDFP Peace Negotiations: Since 1989 Prof. José Maria Sison has been a political consultant of the NDFP in peace negotiations with the GRP. He has advised the NDFP Negotiating Panel in the forging of twelve agreements with its GRP counterpart. These include The Hague Joint Declaration as framework agreement for the peace negotiations, the Joint Agreement on Safety and Immunity Guarantees, the Joint Agreement on Reciprocal Working Committees and the Comprehensive Agreement on Respect for Human Rights and International Humanitarian Law,[9] which fulfills the first of the four items of the substantive agenda in the peace negotiations. However, the GRP-NDFP peace negotiations have been on and off, as result of abrupt demands for NDFP capitulation by the GRP due to the pressure of the reactionary armed forces.

Books and Articles: José Maria Sison is the author of *Struggle for National Democracy* (1967), *Philippine Society and Revolution* (1969),

9 All the signed agreements in the GRP-NDFP peace negotiations are in *The GRP-NDFP Peace Negotiations: Major Agreements and Joint Statements, September 1, 1992-June 9, 2018*, NDFP-Monitoring Committee, 2019.-Editor

Philippine Economy and Politics (2002), *US Terrorism and War in the Philippines* (2003), five volumes of his selected writings from 1968 to 1990, another four volumes from 1991 to 2009, five further volumes from 2009 to 2015 and still further books from year to year. These have provided guidance to the Filipino people's movement for national liberation and democracy.

Prof. Sison has co-authored with Dr. Rainer Werning the book: *The Philippine Revolution: The Leader's View* (1989) and with Ninotchka Rosca, *At Home in the World: Portrait of a Filipino Patriot and Revolutionary* (2004). These should be read to gain a deeper knowledge of his revolutionary ideas and deeds. Prof. Sison's thousands of essays, statements, speeches and interviews have been collected for publication in more 25 volumes according to periods of his life and more than 10 volumes under thematic titles. A complete list of Sison's books is in the next appendix.

List of Books by José Maria Sison

• *Struggle for National Democracy*. Quezon City, Progressive Publications, 1967. [First edition. 280 pages]

• *Patnubay para sa mga kadre at mga kasapi ng Partido Komunista ng Pilipinas*. Ika-3 edisyon, Ang Rebolusyonaryong Paaralan ng kaisipang Mao Tsetung, 1973.

• Guide for Cadres and Members of the Communist Party of the Philippines, Revolutionary School of Mao Zedong Thought, 1969.

• 1. Rectify Errors and Rebuild the Party, Program for a People's Democratic Revolution, Constitution of the Communist Party of the Philippines and Rules of the New People's Army in Guide for Party Cadres and Members, (Somewhere in Luzon: Central Publishing House, 1969). Drafts prepared for the Congress of Reestablishment of the Communist Party of the Philippines on December 26, 1968 and for the organization of the New People's Army on March 29, 1969. [out of print]

• 2. *Philippine Society and Revolution* by Amado Guerrero [nom de guerre] (Manila: Pulang Tala, 1971 and Hongkong: Ta Kung Pao, 1971). 175 pages

• 3. *The First Quarter Storm of 1970* [a compilation of the statements of the chairman of the CPP central committee together with articles and statements by other persons] (Manila: Progressive Publications, 1971) 193 pages.

• 4. Lavaite Propaganda for Revisionism and Fascism; Report of the executive committee to the CPP central committee (Philippines, Central Publishing House, 1972). Draft prepared for and approved by the executive committee. [out of print]

• 5. *Struggle for National Democracy*. 2nd rev. ed., edited by the College Editors' Guild of the Philippines, (Manila: Amado V. Hernandez Foundation, 1972). 200 pages

• 6. *Pomeroy: Portrait of a Revisionist Renegade* (Philippines: Central Publishing House, 1973).

• 7. *Victory to Our People's War: Antirevisionist Essays* (Montreal & Quebec: Red Flag Publications, 1980). Reprints of articles from Ang Bayan.

• 1. *Prison and Beyond; Selected Poems, 1958-1983* (Quezon City: Free José Maria Sison Committee, 1984). A second edition has been published by Asphodel Press, 1986. 130 pages

• 2. Basic Principles of Marxism-Leninism. Unpublished typescript, 1981.

• 1. *Philippine Crisis and Revolution* [Series of ten lectures delivered at the Asian Center of the University of the Philippines, April 15, 1986-May 30, 1986]. (Quezon City: Lagda Publications, 1986). 132 pages

• *Krisis at Rebolusyong Pilipino*: Serye ng mga Lektyur na binigkas ni José Ma. Sison sa Asian Center, University of the Philippines, Abril 15 – Mayo 30, 1986, 132 pages

• 2. *Most Crucial Documents of the Communist Party of the Philippines.* (Tokyo: Renga Publications, 1987). In Japanese.

• 3. *The Philippine Revolution: The Leader's View*, José Maria Sison with Rainer Werning. (New York: Crane Russak, 1989) 260 pages

• Specific Characteristics of our People's War, [Reprint] Utrecht, Christophe Kistler Publications, 2017.

• *US Terrorism and War in the Philippines*, Netherlands, Papieren Tijger, 2003. 133 pages

• *Philippine Economy and Politics*, Co-authored with Julieta de Lima. Philippines, Aklat ng Bayan Inc,1998. 162 pages

• *The Philippine Revolution: The Leader's View.* With Rainer Werning. New York, Crane Russak, 1989.

• *Mao Zedong Thought Lives; Essays in Commemoration of Mao's Centennial,* General Editors: José Maria Sison and Stefan Engel (Center for Social Studies & New Road Publications, 1995). 486 pages.

Selected writings 1968–1991

• Volume 1, 1968-1972, *Foundation for Resuming the Philippine Revolution.* International Network for Philippine Studies and Aklat ng Bayan, Inc., 2013. 435 pages

• Volume 2, 1969-1974, *Defeating Revisionism, Reformism & Opportunism.* International Network for Philippine Studies and Aklat ng Bayan, Inc., 2013. 388 pages

• Volume 3, 1972-1977, *Building Strength through Struggle.* International Network for Philippine Studies and Aklat ng Bayan, Inc., 2013. 547 pages

• Volume 4, 1977-1986, *Detention and Defiance against Dictatorship.* International Network for Philippine Studies and Aklat ng Bayan, Inc., 2013. 664 pages

• Voume 5, 1986-1991, *Continuing the Struggle for National and Social Liberation.* International Network for Philippine Studies and Aklat ng Bayan Inc., 2015. 466 pages

Selected writings 1991–2009

• Volume 1, 1991-1994, *For Justice, Socialism and Peace.* Aklat ng Bayan, Inc., 2009. 214 pages

• Volume 2, 2009. 1995-2001 *For Democracy and Socialism Against Imperialist Globalization.* Aklat ng Bayan, Inc., 2009. 270 pages

• Volume 3, 2001-2006 *Crisis of Imperialism and People's Resistance.* Aklat ng Bayan, Inc., 2009. 269 pages

• Volume 4, 2006-2009, *People's Struggle Against Imperialist Plunder and Terror.* Aklat ng Bayan, Inc., 2009. 269 pages

Peoples' struggles against oppression and exploitation: selected writings 2009–2015

• Volume 1, 2009-2010, *Crisis Generates Resistance.* The Netherlands, International Network for Philippine Studies, 2015. 399 pages

• Volume 2, 2010-2011, *Building People's Power.* The Netherlands, International Network for Philippine Studies, 2016. 482 pages

• Volume 3, 2012, *Combat Neoliberal Globalization.* The Netherlands, International Network for Philippine Studies, 2017. 389 pages

• Volume 4, 2013, *Develop the People's Power.* The Netherlands, International Network for Philippine Studies, 2018. 396 pages

• Volume 5, 2014-15, *Strengthen the People's Struggle against Imperialism and Reaction.* The Netherlands, International Network for Philippine Studies, 2018. 461 pages

Selected writings 2016-

• *People's Resistance to Greed and Terror, Selected Writings, 2016.* The Netherlands, International Network for Philippine Studies, 2018. 433 pages

• *Combat Tyranny and Fascism, Selected Writings, 2017.* The Netherlands, International Network for Philippine Studies, 2019. 461 pages

• *Struggle against Terrorism and Tyranny*, Volume I, January-July 2018, The Netherlands, International Network fopr Philippine Studies, 2019, 433 pages; Volume II, August-December 2018, The Netherlands, International Network for Philippine Studies, 350 pages.

☆ ☆ ☆

Resolution of the Second Congress of the Communist Party of the Philippines

Highest honors to Comrade José Ma. Sison, great communist thinker, leader, teacher and guide of the Filipino proletariat and torch bearer of the international communist movement.

November 7, 2016

The Second Congress of the Communist Party of the Philippines (CPP) extends its profound appreciation and expresses deepest gratitude to Comrade José Ma. Sison for his immense contribution to the Philippine revolution as founding chair of the Party, founder of the New People's Army and pioneer of the People's Democratic Government in the Philippines.

Ka Joma is a Marxist-Leninist-Maoist extraordinaire and indefatigable revolutionary fighter. He applied dialectical and historical materialism to expose the fundamental nature of the semicolonial and semifeudal social system in the Philippines. He put forward an incisive class analysis that laid bare the moribund, exploitative and oppressive rule of the big bourgeois compradors and big landlords in collusion with the US imperialists.

He set forth the program for a people's democratic revolution as immediate preparation for the socialist revolution. He always sets sights on the ultimate goal of communism.

Ka Joma was a revolutionary trailblazer. In his youth, he joined workers' federations and helped organize unions. Ka Joma formed the SCAUP (Student Cultural Association of the University of the Philippines) in 1959 to promote national democracy and Marxism-Leninism and wage ideological and cultural struggle against the religio-sectarians and anti-communist forces among the student intellectuals. Together with fellow proletarian revolutionaries, he initiated study meetings to read and discuss Marxist-Leninist classic writings.

Under Ka Joma's leadership, the SCAUP organized a protest action in March 1961 against the congressional witch hunt of the Committee on Anti-Filipino Activities which targeted UP faculty members accused of writing and publishing Marxist materials in violation of the Anti-Subversion Law. Around 5,000 students joined the first demonstration with an anti-imperialist and anti-feudal character since more than ten years prior. As a consequence, Ka Joma became a target of reactionary violence and survived attempts on his life. Unfazed, he and the SCAUP continued to launch protests against the Laurel-Langley Agreement and the Military Bases Agreement and other issues as land reform and national industrialization, workers rights, civil and political liberties and solidarity with other peoples against US acts of aggression up to 1964.

He and other proletarian revolutionaries eventually joined the old merger Socialist and Communist Party in 1961. In recognition of his communist and youthful fervor, he was assigned to head the youth bureau of the old Party and appointed as member of the executive committee. He initiated meetings to study the classic works of Marx, Lenin, Mao and other great communist thinkers which challenged the stale conditions of the old Party.

He founded the Kabataang Makabayan (KM) in November 1964 and led its development as one of the most important youth organizations in Philippine history. As KM chair, and as a young professor and militant, he went on campus tours and spoke before students as well as young professionals to espouse the necessity of waging a national democratic revolution. His speeches compiled in the volume *Struggle for National Democracy* (SND) served as one of the cornerstones of the national democratic propaganda movement. The KM would eventually be at the head and core of large mass demonstrations during the late 1960s up to the declaration of martial law in 1972.

As one of the leaders of the old party, Ka Joma prepared a political report exposing and repudiating the revisionism and opportunism of the successive Lava leadership as well as the errors of military adventurism and capitulation of the Taruc-Sumulong gang of the old people's liberation army.[10] The old party had deteriorated as an out-and-out revisionist party.

Despite Ka Joma's effort, the old party proved to be beyond resuscitation from its revisionist death. Gangsters in the old party would carry out attempts on his life to snuff the revolutionary revival of the Filipino proletariat.

---

[10] "Rectify Errors and Rebuild the Party" in *Selected Writings, 1968-1991: Foundation for Resuming the Philippine Revolution (1968-1972), 2013, pp. 5-58.* See also *Defeating Revisionism, Reformism and Opportunism (1969-1974)*, 2013.-Editor

As Amado Guerrero, Ka Joma led the reestablishment of the Communist Party of the Philippines on the theoretical foundations of Marxism-Leninism-Maoism. He prepared the Party constitution,[11] the Program for a People's Democratic Revolution[12] and the document Rectify Errors and Rebuild the Party[13] and presided over the Congress of Reestablishment held in Alaminos, Pangasinan on December 26, 1968.

In 1969, he authored *Philippine Society and Revolution* which presents the history of the Filipino people, analyzes the semicolonial and semifeudal character of Philippine society and defines the people's democratic revolution. He prepared the Basic Rules of the New People's Army[14] and the Declaration of the New People's Army[15] and directed the Meeting of Red commanders and fighters to found the New People's Army (NPA) on March 29, 1969.

He led the Party in its early period of growth. He wrote the Organizational Guide and Outline of Reports[16] in April 1971 and the Revolutionary Guide to Land Reform[17] in September 1972 which both served to direct the work of building the mass organizations, organs of political power, units of the people's army and the Party, as well as in mobilizing the peasants in waging agrarian revolution. He authored the Preliminary Report on Northern Luzon[18] in August 1970 which served as a template in the work of other regional committees.

While directing the development and training of the New People's Army from its initial base in Central Luzon to the forests of Isabela in Cagayan Valley, he also guided the youth activists in waging mass struggles in Metro Manila against the US-Marcos dictatorship.

Ka Joma was ever on top of the revolutionary upsurge of the students and workers movement in 1970 and 1971. Chants of Amado Guerrero's name reverberates in Manila and other cities in harmony with calls to join the people's war in the countryside.

---

11 *Selected Writings, 1968-1991: Foundation for Resuming the Philippine Revolution (1968-1972), 2013, pp. 79-93.*-Editor

12 Ibid., *pp. 59-77.*-Editor

13 Ibid., *pp. 5-58.*-Editor

14 Ibid., *pp. 119-132.*-Editor

15 Ibid., *pp. 95-118.*-Editor

16 Ibid., *pp. 313-341.*-Editor

17 Ibid., *pp. 411-424.*-Editor

18 Ibid., *pp. 229-253.*-Editor

The CPP grew rapidly in its first few years under Ka Joma's leadership. The Party established itself across the country and led the nationwide advance of the revolutionary armed struggle. He personally supervised the political and military training of Party cadres and NPA commanders in the forested region of Isabela from where they were deployed to other regions.

In 1971, he presided over the Central Committee and presented the Summing-Up Our Experiences After Three Years (1968-1971).[19] He prepared in 1974 the Specific Characteristics of Our People's War[20] which authoritatively laid out the strategy and tactics for waging people's war in the Philippines. In 1975, he authored Our Urgent Tasks,[21] containing the Central Committee's report and program of action. He served as editor-in-chief of *Ang Bayan* in its first years of publication.

In the underground movement, Ka Joma continued to guide the Party and the NPA in its growth under the brutal fascist martial law regime of dictator Marcos. He issued advisories to underground Party cadres and mass activists. Inspired by the raging people's war in the countryside, they dared the fascist machinery and carried-out organizing efforts among students and workers.

The first workers' strike broke out in 1975 preceding the growth of the workers movement. Large student demonstrations against rising school fees and the deterioration of the educational system were carried out from 1977 onwards completely shattering the terror of martial law.

Ka Joma continued to lead the Party in nationwide growth until 1977 when he and his wife Julie were arrested by the wild dogs of the Marcos dictatorship while in transit from one guerrilla zone to another. He was presented by the AFP to Marcos as a trophy. He was detained, subjected to severe torture, put under solitary confinement for more than five years interrupted only by joint confinement with Julie in 1980-1981, and later partial solitary confinement with one or two other political prisoners from 1982-1985.

While in prison, Ka Joma was able to maintain contact with the Party leadership and revolutionary forces outside through clandestine methods of communication. With the collaboration of Ka Julie, lifelong

---

19 Ibid., *pp. 375-410.*-Editor

20 In *Selected Writings, 1968-1991: Building Strength through Struggle (1972-1977), 2013, pp. 179-217.*-Editor

21 Ibid., *pp. 325-378.*-Editor

partner and comrade of Ka Joma, they produced important letters and advisories. In 1983, Ka Julie released the article JMS On the Mode of Production which served as a theoretical elucidation and clarification of the nature of the semicolonial and semifeudal social system in order to cast away confusion brought about by claims of industrialization by the US-Marcos dictatorship. It counterattacked claims made by pretenders to socialism who insist that the Philippines had become a developing capitalist country under the fascist dictatorship.

A powerful upsurge of the anti-fascist mass movement followed the assassination of Marcos arch rival Benigno Aquino in 1983. This was principally propelled by the workers and student movement which could mount demonstrations of 50,000 or greater from the late 1970s and early 1980s. In 1984, Ka Joma released the paper On the Losing Course of the AFP under the pseudonym Patnubay Liwanag to assess the balance of forces and to signal to or sway the Pentagon to better drop Marcos, which would entail causing a split in the AFP. In September 1984, the Pentagon acceded to the Armacost formula and decided to join the US State Department and other US agencies to drop him. By early 1985 Reagan signed the National Security Directive with definite plan to ease out Marcos.

Ka Joma also asserted the need to weaken the reactionary armed strength in the countryside and expand the people's army to a critical mass 25,000 rifles and one guerrilla platoon per municipality as constructive criticism of the plan to carry out a "strategic counter-offensive."

The anti-fascist upsurge culminated in a people's uprising supported by a military rebellion of elements in the reactionary AFP. The Party's persevering and solid leadership of the anti-fascist movement and revolutionary armed struggle created favorable conditions that led to the overthrow the US-Marcos dictatorship in 1986. Despite strong opposition by the US and reactionary defense establishment, the Aquino regime was compelled to open the detested gates of the Marcos dungeons allowing Ka Joma to be released.

He wasted no time resuming revolutionary work. In a few months time, he mounted a major lecture series to propound a critical class analysis of the Corazon Aquino regime and expose it as representative of big bourgeois comprador and landlord rule. The series of lectures which later comprised the volume *Philippine Crisis and Revolution*[22] countered the "political spectrum" analysis of populists which pictured the Aquino regime as a bourgeois liberal regime to goad the revolutionary forces along the path of class collaboration and capitulation.

These populists as well as other charlatans carried out a campaign to undermine the basic analysis of classes and production system in the Philippines to justify the convoluted concept of a strategic counter-offensive wishfully thinking that the people's war can leapfrog to strategic victory bypassing the probable historical course. A number of key leaders of the Party and revolutionary forces were drawn to the self-destructive path of insurrectionism and premature regularization and military adventurism. This would later bring about grave and almost fatal losses to the Party and the NPA, as well as to the urban mass movement.

Forced to exile in 1987 by the Aquino regime which canceled his passport and travel papers, Ka Joma sought political asylum in The Netherlands while on a lecture tour. He eventually resided in Utrecht and work with other comrades in the international office of the National Democratic Front. Although thousand of miles away from the Philippines, he continued to maintain close contact with the Party leaders in the country and provide advice and guidance to help them in their work.

Ka Joma served as one of the steadfast exponent of the Second Great Rectification Movement launched by the 10th Plenum of the CPP Central Committee in 1992. The Party leadership actively sought Ka Joma's theoretical insights and analysis. In preparing the key document Reaffirm Our Basic Principles and Rectify Errors,[23] the Party leadership referred to Ka Joma and the Party's founding documents which he authored. With Ka Joma's full support, the rectification campaign of 1992-1998 united and strengthened the Party to ever greater heights.

---

22 In *Selected Writings, 1968-1991: Continuing the Struggle for National and Social Liberation (1986-1991), 2013, pp. 61-141.*-Editor

23 *Rebolusyon;* Theoretical and Political Journal of the Central Committee of the Communist Party of the Philippines, Special Issue 1, January 1993.-Editor

Ka Joma also played a key role in authoring the paper Stand for Socialism Against Modern Revisionism[24] which illuminated the path of socialist revolution during the dark hours of the complete restoration of capitalism in the Soviet Union in 1990 touted in the monopoly bourgeois mass media as the fall of socialism, a refutation of communism, and the "end of history" and final victory of the capitalist system.

Reflecting Ka Joma's sharp Maoist critique of modern revisionism, the paper presented a clear historical understanding of the process of capitalist restoration in the USSR from 1956 onwards. This served as key to understanding the continuing viability of socialism and to inspiring the Filipino proletariat to persevere in the two-stage revolution and the international proletariat to carry forward the socialist cause.

Ka Joma's Utrecht base eventually became a political center of the international communist and anti-imperialist resistance movements. He played an important role in the centennial celebration of Mao Zedong in 1993 which served as a vigorous ideological campaign to reaffirm Marxist-Leninist views and to proclaim Maoism as the third epochal development of Marxism-Leninism.

Up to the early 2000s, he also played a lead role in the formation of the International Conference of Marxist-Leninist Parties and Organizations (ICMLPO) which serves as a center for ideological and practical exchange among communist and workers parties which stood for socialism and opposed modern revisionism. He provided valuable insights and practical assistance to numerous communist parties from Asia to Europe and the Americas.

Over the past decade, he has led the International League of Peoples' Struggles or the ILPS which has served as coordinating center for anti-imperialist movements around the globe.[25] He authored the paper "On Monopoly Capitalist 'Globalization'"[26] in 1996 which

---

24 *Rebolusyon*; Theoretical and Political Journal of the Central Committee of the Communist Party of the Philippines, No.2, April-June; Series 1992.-Editor

25 Most of the statements and messages issued as ILPS Chairperson have been collected in *People's Struggles against Oppression and Exploitation, Selected Writings, 2009-2015*, 5 volumes.-Editor

26 In *Selected Writings of José Ma. Sison, 1991-2009: Volume 2, For Democracy and Socialism against Imperialism and Globalization*, pp. 59-79.-Editor

clarified that the proletariat remains in the era of imperialism and socialist revolution.

Because of his role in guiding the advance of the international anti-imperialist struggle, Ka Joma was put in the crosshairs of US imperialism. He was included in the US list of "foreign terrorists," together with the CPP and NPA. At 68 years old, he was arrested in 2007 by the Dutch police and detained for more than 15 days.

Since 1992, together with the NDFP Negotiating Panel, Ka Joma has also ably represented the interests of the Filipino people and revolutionary movement in peace negotiations with successive representatives of the Government of the Republic of the Philippines (GRP). He was appointed as Chief Political Consultant of the NDFP Negotiating Panel and has deftly guided it in negotiations with the GRP over the past 25 years.

Over the past several years, Ka Joma continued to provide invaluable insights into the domestic crisis and the situation of the revolutionary forces. He continues to provide advice to the Party and the revolutionary forces in the Philippines on resolving the problems of advancing the revolution to a new and higher stage.

He has set forth critical analyses of the objective international conditions. He has put forward a Marxist-Leninist critique of the capitalist crisis of overproduction which is at the base of the international financial crisis and the prolonged depression that has wracked the global capitalist system. He has reaffirmed that we are still at the historical epoch of imperialism, the last crisis stage of capitalism.

Ka Joma is the torch bearer of the international communist movement. Through the dark period of capitalist restoration, he has kept the flames of Marxism-Leninism-Maoism burning and inspired the proletariat to take advantage of the crisis of global capitalism, persevere along the path of socialism and communism and bring the international communist revolution to a new chapter of revival and reinvigoration.

Resolutions:

The Second Congress of the Communist Party of the Philippines (CPP) resolves to give the highest honors to Comrade José Ma. Sison, great communist thinker, leader, teacher and guide of the Filipino proletariat and torch bearer of the international communist movement.

In recognition of Ka Joma's immense contribution to the Philippine revolution and the international workers movement, the Second Congress further resolves:

1. to instruct the Central Committee to continue to seek Ka Joma's insights and advice on various aspects of the Party's work in the ideological, political and organizational fields.

2. to endorse the five-volume writings of José Ma. Sison as basic reference and study material of the CPP and to urge the entire Party membership and revolutionary forces to read and study Ka Joma's writings.

The Second Congress of the Communist Party of the Philippines (CPP) is certain that with the treasure of Marxist-Leninist-Maoist work that Ka Joma has produced over the past five decades of revolutionary practice, the Party is well-equipped in leading the national democratic revolution to greater heights and complete victory in the coming years.

On the Designation of José Maria Sison as Chairperson Emeritus of the International League of Peoples' Struggle

Resolution of the ILPS Sixth International Assembly

Recalling that José Maria Sison was the Chairperson of the International Initiative Committee that conceptualized and prepared the International League of Peoples' Struggle (ILPS) from 1998 to 2001 and founded it in 2001,

Considering that he presided over the First International Assembly that founded the ILPS in 2001 and subsequently served as the General Consultant of the ILPS from 2001 to 2004,

Recognizing his services for five terms or 15 years as Chairperson of the ILPS International Coordinating Committee from the Second to the Sixth International Assembly, or 2004 to 2019,

Appreciating and honoring him for all the foregoing and valuing highly his continued connection with and further contributions to the ILPS,

We hereby designate Prof. José Maria Sison as Chairperson Emeritus of the ILPS, upon the end of his current term as Chairperson of the International Coordinating Committee.

As such, he may be consulted and requested to give advice to the ILPS Chairperson or any ILPS leading organ. He may also take initiative to give advice to the aforementioned. Whenever appropriate, he may be invited to address or grace important events of ILPS.

Done at the Sixth International Assembly of the International League of Peoples' Struggle in Hong Kong on June 23, 2019.

☆ ☆ ☆

Tribute to José Maria Sison

Read at the ILPS Solidarity Night, June 27, 2019

By Lisa Ito, Concerned Artists of the Philippines[27]

Like other Filipinos of petty-bourgeois origins, the first time I heard the name José Maria Sison was in school during the late 1990s. By then, he was the country's most prominent political refugee. He was already based in the Netherlands for almost a decade since he fought the Marcos dictatorship and survived imprisonment, including torture and solitary confinement. Attuned to the pulse and political developments of the Philippines, he represented a mass movement flourishing long before our generation was even born.

My contemporaries came of age during EDSA II in 2000. This was the second People Power revolt which ousted President. Joseph Estrada and which was followed by regimes that were all enablers of the neoliberal order. Through progressive organizations, institutions, and individuals and his media exchanges with state propaganda and government officials, we who never lived through the darkest years of the Marcos dictatorship were introduced to Ka Joma as a thinker, peace consultant, cultural worker, poet, propagandist.

As a student, I was then pursuing research on histories of protest art and sought his insights to questions through email. Years later, the chance to meet in person was opened through initiatives of artists and cultural workers in Europe who responded positively to the acts of radical imagination, put into practice, that Ka Joma represented. Always, Ka Joma and others make the most of these instances and opportunities: turning non events and idle spells into educational discussions and learning moments for all.

There is a saying in Tagalog: "walang kapaguran," which can be translated to tireless or indefatigable. I think this observation can be well extended to the work of organizations like the ILPS and

---

27 The Concerned Artists of the Philippines is an organization of artists, musicians, writers, filmmakers and cultural workers working towards a nationalist, people-oriented art and culture. Among its founders in 1983 were National Artists Lino Brocka and Ishmael Bernal and it was in the forefront of the anti-dictatorship struggle that eventually led to the downfall of the Marcos dictatorship.-Editor

movements that he led: whose drive is honed by discipline and fuelled by a commitment to "seize the day and seize the hour," no matter how difficult or insurmountable the circumstances or challenges.

We have a lot to learn from Ka Joma's life and practice, shared through forms such as films, interviews, and anthologies. As Filipino activists, our lives have definitely been influenced by texts he has produced, which range from essays such as *Philippine Society and Revolution*, *Struggle for National Democracy,* to poems such as those in *Prison and Beyond*. I hope more people—including anti-imperialist youth, students, teachers, and organizers involved in the task of consciousness-raising among the people—will have similar chances to interact with him and other such comrades as well. At the very least, he has inspired me to try to be a better teacher, a better cultural worker, and a better person.

A few months ago, Ka Julie de Lima wrote about the importance of the "pen and the gun" (2018), the cultural and military fronts, in the continuing Philippine revolution since 1968. Ka Joma embodies this interface in how he successfully overcome threats to his life and safety, legal and political persecution, terrorist listing, harassment, black propaganda, intrigue, and fake news.

We should learn from how Ka Joma FIGHTS BACK against these ATTACKS. Even today, he shifts between discussions of literature to political analysis, poetic form to videoke or other modes of entertainment, public lectures and video speeches to spontaneous verbal jousts and Facebook posts to convey important messages. I can only imagine how he will take to using Twitter!

Tonight, we honor one of the most beloved figures of the continuing Philippine revolution and the global fight against imperialism. But his is also a face which also embodies the stories, lives and sacrifices of countless other revolutionaries and comrades, including the martyred, the disappeared, and those who continue to be part of the struggle today.

In paying tribute to Ka Joma we also pay tribute to millions of other extraordinary comrades, all fighting for a system that upholds dignity, labor, and social justice for all the ordinary people who hold up the world.

Thank you, Ka Joma, for teaching generations of activists how revolutionary struggle for national liberation and global solidarity against empire is possible, real, and most of all, truly joyful. Mabuhay po kayo!

Poems

1

Sometimes the Heart Yearns for Mangoes

March 30, 1994

Sometimes, the heart yearns
For mangoes where there are apples,
For orchids where there are tulips,
For warmth, where it is cold,
For mountainous islands,
Where there is flatland.

Far less than the home,
And the flow of kith and kin,
Unfamiliar and now familiar
Things and places trigger
The pain of sundered relations,
Of losses by delays and default.

Direct dialing, fax machines,
Computer discs and video casettes
And visitors on jumbo jets,
Fail to close the gap
Between rehearsed appearances
And the unrehearsed life at home.

There are colleagues and friends
That make a strange land loveable.
But they have their routines,
Their own lives to live,
Beyond the comprehension
And pertinence of the stranger.

Those who seek to rob the exile
Of home, kith and kin,
Of life, limb and liberty
Are the loudest to mock at him
Who is helplessly at sea,
Uprooted from his soil.

The well-purposed exile continues
To fight for his motherland
Against those who banished him,
The unwelcomed exploiters of his people,
And is certain that he is at home
In his own country and the world.

* * *

2

My Pen and My Tongue

Maximum Security Prison
Scheveningen, The Hague
September 4, 2007

The only weapons I have
Are my pen and my tongue
To protest greed and terror
And call for people's resistance
In my Motherland and in the world.

I protest the daily violence
Of exploiting the toiling masses
And burying them in poverty,
Misery, slow death and silence.
I call for ending the pillage.

I protest the wars of aggression
And all acts of repression
That perpetuate exploitation
By the imperialists and puppets.
I call for ending the carnage.

I fight for human rights and just peace
In solidarity with all peoples
And I praise and encourage them
To wage the just struggle
For national and social liberation.

The imperialists and the puppets
React to my pen and tongue
With false charges, demonization
And the iron fist of state power.
But I stand with the people.

3

The Giant Oak
(Tribute to Comrade Mao Zedong)

December 26, 1993

In the bitterness of winter
The giant oak stands erect,
A hundred years old,
A tower of countless seasons.
The mayflies of summer
Are no match to the oak
And the merciless cold.

He who has departed
But whose spirit lives on
And cannot be exorcised
By all sorts of sorcerers
Is sometimes carved out
From a branch of the oak
In the image of his foes
For rituals to steal
The magic of his name.
There are the kisses of betrayal
On the parchment,
Droning incantations of sacrilege
And myths of infamy
Against his great memory.

When foes are haunted
By his thoughts and deeds
They are in mortal fear
Of the living force inspired
For the bigger battles ahead,
As the light and darkness
Clash in the horizon
And as the best and the worst
Are driven to define themselves.

* * *

4

US Is the Terrorist Monster

August 2013

The US has not yet paid for the blood debt
In killing 1.5 million of the Filipino people
And has not cared to give even an apology
As it continues to violate their sovereignty
And enjoy the bounty of successful aggression
And treachery with impunity and utmost arrogance.

The Filipino people have suffered the terrorism
Of US imperialism for so long, as if without end,
And with the help of its puppet accomplices,
It designates as terrorist and further represses
The victims and the revolutionary forces
Who fight for national and social liberation.

Empires have come and gone in history.
US imperialism and capitalism are not eternal.
The people strive to undercut and topple
The power of the system that oppresses them.
The people cannot accept the terrorist monster
Maligning as terrorist their heroes and forces.

5

The Master Puppeteer and the Puppets

August 2013

In neocolonial times, the master puppeteer
Lends the puppets grandeur and puts them on stage
In the mass media and all kinds of gatherings.
To conjure the illusion of democracy, he arranges
The electoral contests like dazzling cock fights
In so many town fiestas for several months.

But most important to the master puppeteer
Is to elect the puppet politicians that serve best
The collaboration of the US and local exploiters,
And make the exploited and oppressed believe
That they have freely chosen the best of possible.
Thus, the US has prolonged its domination.

But the revolutionary movement has arisen
To arouse, organize and mobilize the masses,
To confront the oppressors and exploiters,
To seize power wave upon wave in the localities
And gain strength for the liberation of the nation
And mainly the workers and peasants.

The Filipino people shun the master puppeteer
For rotating puppet rulers to oppress them,
They reject the blatant despotism of Marcos
As well as the pseudo-democratic successors
Who take turns at oppressing the people
And serving the foreign and local exploiters.

★ ★ ★

6

The Way to a Just Peace

December 2005

The Yanks came posing as a friend
Then they unleashed aggression
To rape, plunder and imprison
Our long suffering motherland.
The way to a just peace is to fight
For national liberation

By ceaseless, ruthless use of arms
The ruling classes dominate,
Oppress and exploit the people
Mainly the workers and peasants.
The way to a just peace is to fight
For social liberation

The people must rise up to fight
The imperialists and puppets
Gain the power to free themselves
And build a just and lasting peace

The kind of peace that the imperialists
And the local exploiting classes wish
Is the abject surrender of the people
To the daily violence of exploitation.
The way to a just peace is to end
The violence of exploitation

Build a just and lasting peace!

☆ ☆ ☆

7

Monsters in the Market

February 1, 2012

Shame on those who spread the false illusion
Of the free market and tout the law of the jungle.
The self-interest of monopolies is so visible,
A hand that squeezes and ruins the lives of people.

Monopolies are monsters preying on the market.
They can't hide their greed with any sleight of hand.
They make super-profits from the sweat and blood
Of entire nations, the workers and the peasants.

Awake and arise, unite to fight the monsters
That oppress and exploit the people
In the factories, farms and marketplace.
Let us free ourselves and build a new world.

8

The Monster Ravages the Forests and Mountains

August 2013

The birds have fled and sing no more
Where the monster has felled the trees
With complete abandon, with no concern
For the life of the forest that he ravages.

The wooden furniture and panelings
Of homes and offices in cities are splendid
While the folks where the trees are gone
Miss the savor of wild plants and animals.

And the flood and drought take turns
In drowning and parching the land
To ruin the rhythm and future of crops
And afflict the folks on lower ground.

The monster is frenzied at ripping off
The mineral ores from the mountains.
He digs wide open pits and uses chemicals
Of the deadliest sorts to hasten the extraction.

The monster is pleased with the gold,
Silver, platinum, nickle, chrome, zink, copper
And other ores to feed his industry
And make all sorts of strong and shiny things.

While poison flows to the streams and wells,
The tailings silt and choke the rivers,
And the mountains erode until they crumble
With landslides and mud flows to afflict the folks.

By denuding the forests, the monster robs
The land of its lungs and the shield against typhoons.
By extracting the ores, he robs the country
Of its development independent of its greed.

9

Once More Solitary Confinement

September 2007

At the peak of our youth,
Full of romance and vigor,
We were imprisoned for a long time
In a small and stifling cell
Of solitary confinement by the dictatorship
Where time was a turtle
As if we had no more hope
To be free from the steel door,

We were separated, my love.
And in extreme loneliness
My heart always cried out
Then we come together again.
Loneliness and hope merged
In my fighting poems.
And in the long run, we came together
Upon the overthrow of the dictatorship.

Now that we are of mature age
Our resolve is more the ever firm
But the body is fragile
And accustomed to your care
Once more I am imprisoned
In a small and stifling cell
Of solitary confinement by the imperialists.
It looks like I will be finished here.

We are once more separared from each other
And in extreme loneliness
My heart is always crying out
That we come together again
Loneliness and hope merge
In my fighting songs.
We come together again in the movement
And in the fulfillment of our legacy to the people.

10

Stages of My Life

September 2007

If you trace the course
And the stages of my life,
The story is quite simple,
Easy to recall with the head and heart.

In the spring of my life,
I observed the hardship
Of the toiling masses around.
My heart and spirit was moved.

In the summer of my life,
I decided to fight
The oppressors and exploiters.
I was tempered in the flames of struggle.

In the autumn of my life,
I can see the wide scope
And the strong advance
Of the masses on fertile soil.

In the winter of my life,
I always feel from the field
The flames of struggle.
I am sure of the victory of the people.

☆ ☆ ☆

11

Welcome the Unwelcome

November 3, 2018

Long before you come,
You rattle your sabres
Made in some alien land,
You boast of your ill intent
Against the toiling masses.
Come as you please
In whatever strength,
We watch your parade
From the simple and easy start
To the complex and difficult paths.
Our welcome is even readier
When we hear your air power
Thundering and stirring the winds
And the rumbling of trucks
Before you can creep on us.
We see your columns in advance
And if we are unable to make
A crowded grand reception,
We make a simple welcome
Without ceremony for you.
But there can be tokens of welcome
To our alluring home ground,
Outbursts from the roadside
And under your wheels and feet
And precision shots from wherever.
If still your strength is such
That you can encamp long,
We will continue the fireworks
To make you dance, lose sleep
And get worn out before you leave.
When you decide to leave,
We gladly take our turn to close in

And give you the biggest fireworks
Of farewell and thank you
For leaving gifts to us.
While you focus on small parts
Of our wide home ground,
We can take full initiative
And choose your weak points
Somewhere else to wipe them out.
On any day or any night,
We can tickle your weak point
To lure you into a grand reception
Along the most perilous routes
Or to hit another point beyond your guess.
Why do we welcome the unwelcome?
You bring to us what we need,
You save us time and sweat
To collect the means to become stronger
Before seizing your palace in the city.

12

The Long Struggle for Freedom

December 26, 2018
Dedicated to the 50th annniversary
of the founding of the Communist Party of the Philippines

It took more than 300 years
For the Filipino nation to take shape
And shake off the colonial yoke
In hundreds of uprisings
Until the Katipunan and the people
Defeated the foe and won their freedom.
Since the imperialist bird of prey
Cast its shadow and dug its claws
On our beloved motherland,
It has been more than 100 years
That the people have continued to fight
For national and social liberation.
The last 50 years of the struggle
Has been most fruitful:
The revolutionary party of the proletariat,
The people's army, the united front,
The mass movement of the oppressed
And the people's government.
All these are ever growing in the archipelago
And advancing in waves against the foe
That rules the ever rotting system
Of greed and terror
And serves foreign masters
That the people of the world detest.
We see the rising trend of revolution
Amidst the crisis in the country and abroad
That inflicts intolerable suffering
And drives the people to struggle harder
For their soonest freedom from tyranny
And a bright future in socialism.

We struggle long for freedom,
We never give up no matter how long.
But we seize every moment
To strike a blow against the foe
And hasten the day of our liberation
From all oppression and exploitation.

13

Which Shall Come Ahead?

Utrecht, October 16, 2018

Which shall come ahead?
The blazing of forests,
The thawing of icebergs,
The rise of oceans,
The drowning of cities,
The parching of the land,
The whimpering death?

Which shall come ahead?
Sudden fright at the big burst,
Mushrooms in the sky,
Blinding light in a trice,
Before the endless night
Under the seamless fog,
The freezing of the land?

Which shall come ahead?
The endless rule and lure of greed,
The cycles of boom and bust,
The captive flow of blood and sweat,
The ruin of the greenscape,
Or the breaking of chains
To end myths of the endless?

Which shall come ahead?
The rise of the human spirit,
The liberation of the oppressed,
To smite the vile sources
Of greed, wars and plunder
To end the absurd choice
Of calamity to doom all humankind.

* * *

14

I Wish to Be Taken for Granted

November 5, 2013

I wish to be taken for granted
Like the wind that you breathe
Like the sunlight on your face
Like the ground at your feet
Like the water that you drink.

I wish to be taken for granted
Like birdsong lofted by the breeze
Like wood on fire for your comfort
Like the grass greening the field
Like the silent swan afloat on the pond.

I wish to be taken for granted
Like the workers in the factories
Like the tillers in the farms
Like those who dwell in schools
Like those who recreate the world.

I wish to be taken for granted
But I shall smile with satisfaction
If some people sometimes remember
That I did what I could in my time
To add to what is now commonplace.

One new generation after another
Shall create new ideas and new things
To surpass the feats of the past
There are no limits but the sky,
The sun, the earth and the waters.

* * *

Photographs

Photographs Relevant to Chapter I

Figure 1. Rainer Werning gifts Jose Maria Sison a rare copy of his German translation of the latter's book, *Philippine Society and Revolution*.

Figure 2. Visiting Tony Benn, Left-wing Labour MP, at his London home, March 1987. He took up progressive issues and was a great admirer of Mao Zedong, describing him as "one of the greatest—if not the greatest—figures of 20th century.

Figure 3. At the Sandino Museum in Managua, Nicaragua in 1988.

Figure 4. With Luis Jalandoni and responsible comrades (including Tania Maceda and Gilda Vasallos) of the International Department of the Communist Party of Cuba in 1988.

Figure 5. In front of the Frank Pais bronze statue on the hill overlooking the entrance of Santiago de Cuba.

Figure 6. At the Red Fort in New Delhi, India on second travel to India in September 1988.

Photographs Relevant to Chapter II to V

Figure 7. Presiding over the International Seminar on Mao Zedong Thought at the celebration marking Mao's 100th birth anniversary sponsored by the International Conference of Marxist-Leninist Parties and Organizations held in Botrop, Germany in 1993.

Figure 8. With renowned Dutch economist Prof. dr. Arnold Heertje at the Forum on the Global Economic and Financial Crisis on January 30, 2009 at De Balie, Amsterdam.

Figure 9. Speaking before the Marxian Study Group, Institute of Social Studies, The Hague, Little AULA, 9 March 2011.

Figure 10. Lecturing on the Development, Current Status and Prospects of Maoist Theory and Practice in the Philippines at the Conference on Maoism at Jan van Eyck Academie, Maastricht. September 5, 2012.

Figure 11. With Leila Khaled, prominent leader of the Popular Front for the Liberation of Palestine.

Figure 12. Lecturing to Students on Political Mobilization at the Institute of Conflict Studies, University of Utrecht on December 6, 2010.

Figure 13. Delivering the keynote address at the New World Summit, second session on "The National Liberation Movement in the Philippines and 'Terrorist' Listing by Foreign Powers" held in Leiden on December 31, 2012.

Photographs Relevant to Chapter VI

Figure 14. With Nick Scheerder as he presides over an asylum support committee meeting in October 1988.

Figure 15. With lawyers in Sison v. Marcos Estate in the US. Photo taken after Jose Maria Sison and Julieta de Lima made their depositions against Marcos in Utrecht in 1991. L to R: Atty. Romeo T. Capulong of Public Interest Law Center, Ralph G. Steinhardt III and lead lawyer Paul L. Hoffman of American Civil Liberties Union, Jose Maria Sison and Ellen Lutz of Human Rights Watch.

Figure 16. At press conference with lawyers announcing filing of case vs EU terrorist listing at The Hague, December 12, 2002.

Figure 17. At the European Court of Justice in Luxemburg.

Figure 18. On the way to Court of First Instance hearing with lawyer Bernard Tomlow, Luis G. Jalandoni and lead lawyer Jan Fermon.

Figure 19. Press Conference after favorable European Court of First Instance decision against the terrorist listing of Jose Maria Sison on September 30, 2009.

Figure 20. Defense lawyers Michiel Pestman and Ties Prakken at hearing of false murder charge against Sison in The Hague, November 2007.

Figure 21. Thanking former US Attorney General Ramsey Clark, for his support as Chairman of the International Action Center for leading the US campaign against Sison's terrorist listing.

Photographs Relevant to Chapter VII

Figure 22. Signing The Hague Joint Declaration on September 1, 1992.

Figure 23. At the signing of the Comprehensive Agreement on Respect for Human Rights and International Humanintarian Law (CARHRIHL) in The Hague on March 16, 1998.

Figure 24. On a phone conversation with President Fidel Ramos after the signing of the CARHRIHL on March 16, 1998.

Figure 25. Resumption of formal talks in the GRP-NDFP peace negotiations at beginning of the presidency of Gloria Arroyo at the Holmenkollen Hotel in Oslo, Norway on April 27, 2001, a few months after the ouster of Estrada on January 22, 2001.

Figure 26. NDFP negotiating panel with consultants & staff in Oslo for the February 2011 resumption of the formal talks in the peace negotiations with the government of President Benigno Aquino III.

Figure 27. At the press conference of the launch of the NDFP International Legal Advisory Team (ILAT) at the NDFP International Information Office in Utrecht on November 3, 2011.

Figure 28. NDFP Negotiating Panel members in consultations with the International Legal Advisory Team: Ann Morris of the Haldane Society of Socialist Lawyers (3rd fr L), Edre Olalia of the National Union of Peoples' Lawyers (6th fr L), and Jan Fermon of the International Association Democratic Lawyers (7th fr L).

Figure 29. Philippine Ecumenical Peace Platform delegation visits NDFP negotiating panel in July 2015.

Figure 30. At the reopening of GRP-NDFP formal peace talks at Holmenkollen hotel in Oslo, Norway in August 2016 with the few released JASIG protected consultants of the NDFP negotiating panel.

Figure 31. Last successful formal talks between the GRP and NDFP negotiating panels before these were terminated by the GRP president. The meetings were held in Noordwijk aan Zee, The Netherlands on April 3-6, 2017.

Photographs Relevant to Chapter VIII

Figure 32. Delivering keynote address at NDFP 45th anniversary celebration in Amsterdam on April 21, 2018 2018.

Figure 33. Speaking at the International CPP 50th Anniversary Celebration held at the Basis voor Actuale Kunst in Utrecht on December 29, 2018.

Figure 34. Poster for the 50th CPP Founding Anniversary Celebration: The future is bright for the Filipino people's struggle for national and social liberation!

Figure 35. Delivering the keynote address at the New People's Army 50th anniversary celebration in Amsterdam on March 31, 2019.

Photographs Relevant to Chapter IX

Figure 36. Presiding at Founding Assembly of the International League of Peoples' Struggle at Zutphen in the Netherlands in May 2001. Audience of delegates is below.

Figure 37. ILPS May 20 protest against NATO 2012 Summit on May 20-21, 2012.

Figure 38. ILPS May Day protest march in Rotterdam on May 1, 2014.

Figure 39. Keynoting the study conference to celebrate in advance the 100th anniversary of the October Revolution in Amsterdam, The Netherlands on September 23, 2017.

Figure 40. Presiding over the ILPS International Coordinating Committee meeting on March 16, 2019.

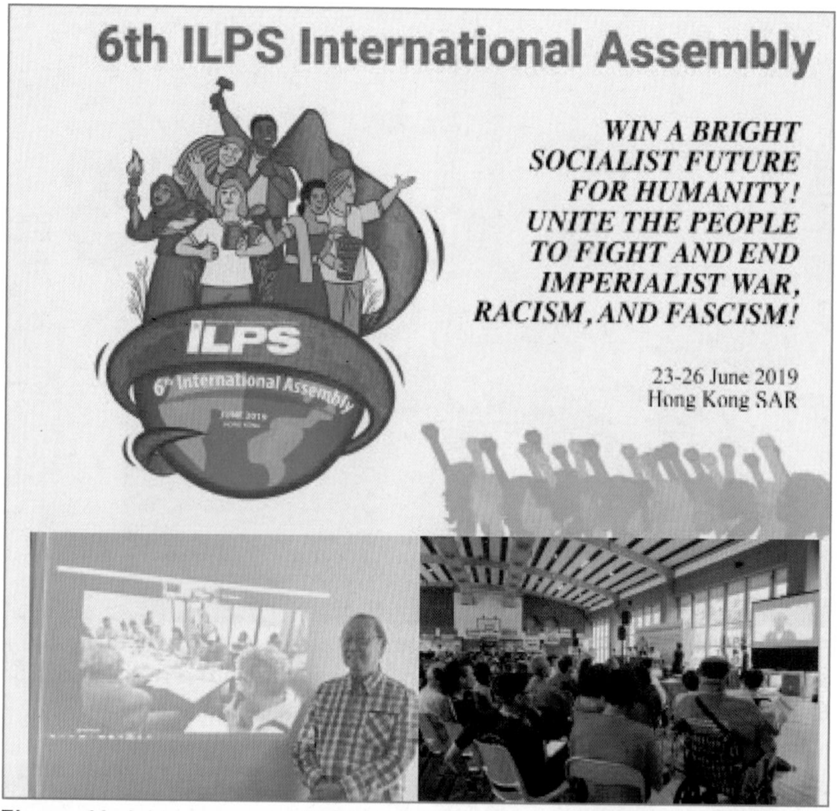
6th ILPS International Assembly
WIN A BRIGHT SOCIALIST FUTURE FOR HUMANITY! UNITE THE PEOPLE TO FIGHT AND END IMPERIALIST WAR, RACISM, AND FASCISM!
23-26 June 2019
Hong Kong SAR
ILPS
6th International Assembly

Figure 41. Addressing via ZOOM the ILPS 6th International Assembly.

PEOPLE OF THE WORLD, UNITE!
Defeat imperialism!
LONG LIVE
international solidarity!

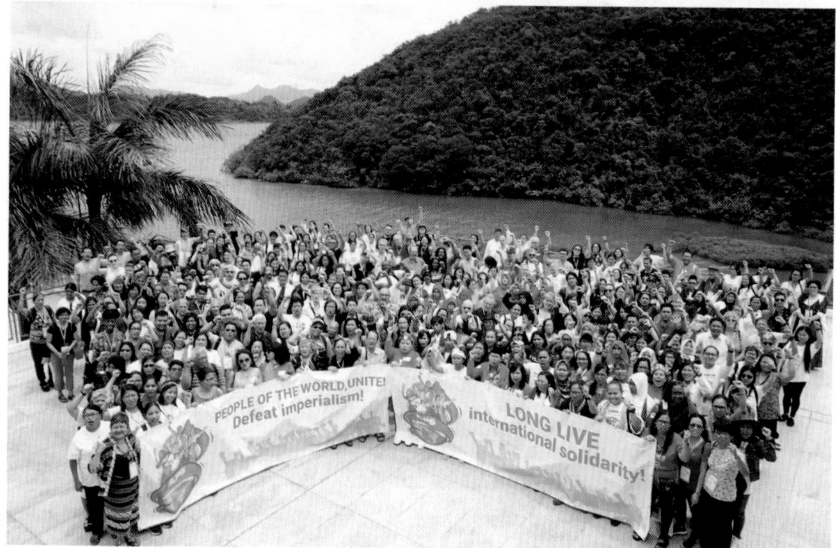

Figure 42. Group picture of delegates to the ILPS 6th General Assembly.

Photographs Relevant to Chapter X

Figure 43. Revolutionary and poet Jose Maria Sison receives the Southeast Asia WRITE Award in Bangkok, Thailand in October 1986 for his book of poetry, *Prison and Beyond* from then Crown Prince and now King Maha Vajiralongkorn. The SEA Write award is the highest literary award in Southeast Asia.

Figure 44. Poetry reading at the Poetry Park in Rotterdam in June 1994.

Figure 45. At launch of *The Guerrilla Is Like a Poet* at the New World Academy in November 2013.

Figure 46. At book launch of *At Home in the World* during the ILPS 2nd International Assembly in Eindhoven, the Nethrlands on November 12, 2004.

Figure 47. At the launch of *Detention and Defiance against Dictatorship* and commemoration of the International Day of Solidarity with Political Prisoners at the NDFP International Office on December 3, 2014

Figure 48. The Musical *Mandirigma'y Makata; Makata'y Mandirigma* (The Warrior Is a Poet; the Poet is a Warrior) staged on November 30, 2007 to honor Sison for his 50 years of service to the Filipino people's struggle for national freedom and democracy. The DVD video recording of the stage play is available for sale at the NDFP International Information Office.

JOMA SISON AND KARL MEDINA. MEDINA WON THE BEST ACTOR AWARD IN THE 2013 CINEFILIPINO FILM FESTIVAL FOR PLAYING SISON IN THE MOVIE, THE GUERRILLA IS A POET

Figure 49. Poster of the movie *The Guerrilla Is a Poet*. On the left is Sison and on the right is the actor Karl Medina who plays him.

Figure 50. Sison Portrait in oil done in February 2011 by master artist Rafael Maniago who is based in California, USA. Maniago has painted the portraits of Southeast Asian leaders.

Figure 51. *Focus on Jose Maria Sison,* mural by prominent Filipino social realist artist Pablo Baens Santos, February 2015.

Figure 52. Palestinian activist-painter Mustapha Awad painting Sison's portrait at the NDFP International Information Office on February 7, 2016.

Figure 53. Poster designed for the ILPS 6th IA program honoring ILPS Chairperson upon his retirement.

Figure 54. Logo for ILPS Resolution designating Jose Maria Sison as ILPS Chairperson Emeritus.